The Art of the

BURGER

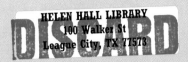

HELEN HALL LIBRARY
100 Walker St
League City, TX 77573

DISCARD

D0580319

OCT 1 5

The Art of the

BURGER

More Than 50 Recipes to Elevate America's Favorite Meal to Perfection

RECIPES BY JENS FISCHER

PHOTOGRAPHS BY MARIA BRINKOP

TRANSLATION BY MICHAEL SPIETH

Skyhorse Publishing

HELEN HALL LIBRARY
City of League City
100 West Walker
League City, TX 77573-3899
DISCARD

© 2014 Neuer Umschau Buchverlag
Translation copyright © 2015 by Skyhorse
Publishing, Inc.

First published in 2014 under the title of THE
ART OF BURGER by Neuer Umschau
Buchverlag GmbH, Moltkestrasse 14, 67433
Neustadt/Weinstrasse, Germany.

All rights reserved. No part of this book may be
reproduced in any manner without the express
written consent of the publisher, except in the case
of brief excerpts in critical reviews or articles. All
inquiries should be addressed to Skyhorse
Publishing, 307 West 36th Street, 11th Floor, New
York, NY 10018.

Skyhorse Publishing books may be purchased in
bulk at special discounts for sales promotion,
corporate gifts, fund-raising, or educational
purposes. Special editions can also be created to
specifications. For details, contact the Special Sales
Department, Skyhorse Publishing, 307 West 36th
Street, 11th Floor, New York, NY 10018 or info@
skyhorsepublishing.com.

Skyhorse® and Skyhorse Publishing® are registered
trademarks of Skyhorse Publishing, Inc.®, a
Delaware corporation.

Visit our website at www.skyhorsepublishing.com.
10 9 8 7 6 5 4 3 2

Library of Congress Cataloging-in-Publication
Data is available on file.

Cover design by Brian Peterson

Print ISBN: 978-1-63220-508-7
Ebook ISBN: 978-1-63220-751-7

Printed in the United States of America

RECIPES
Jens Fischer, Monzingen, Germany

PHOTOS AND STYLING
Maria Brinkop, Hildesheim, Germany
www.fotobrinkop.de

TRANSLATION
Michael Spieth, New York, New York

FOOD STYLING
Thomas Lauterbach, Hamburg, Germany
www.lauterbachfood.de

**IMAGE COMPOSITION OF FLYING BUR-
GERS ON PAGES 40, 51, 69, 76, 99, 102, 108
AND 122**
Markus von Lücken, Hannover, Germany
www.bildbotschaft.de

DESIGN
Wagner Rexin Gestaltung, Dirk Wagner,
Stutensee

THANKS TO
- The Könneker steam bakery of Hildesheim,
  Germany, for supplying the burger buns.
- The Bionatic company for the biodegradable
  packaging for the image of the burger "Big in
  Japan" (page 127).

CONTENTS

MOVE IN THE RIGHT DIRECTION
AND YOU'LL BE ON THE RIGHT TRACK!

In any city around the world you can find a burger twenty-four hours a day on virtually every corner—walk-up, drive-in, sliders, double size, super size, king size, and countless other variations on unimaginative, standardized fast food burgers from under the heat lamp. But there is another way . . .

The Art of the Burger is much more than just a burger recipe book; it is inspiration and a creative jolt for those who want more: innovative patties, inventive bun choices, imaginative toppings, creative preparation, and of course, more flavor! Making good choices is everything, and that's why these tips won't just make your burger complete, but will make it an unchallenged hit.

ACTOR IN LEADING ROLE—THE PATTY

Without quality, nothing works. This applies in particular to the most important part of the burger: the patty. Whether classic beef, hearty pork, or extravagant fish, the ingredients' freshness is always the top priority! You won't find it in the freezer section of the supermarket. The best will be from a local butcher or fish market. And for those making vegetarian patties from grains, you don't have to go to your local farm. Find quality grains at a natural foods store or a well-stocked grocery store.

🐄 BEEF

The classic patty is made of beef. Shoulder, neck pieces, or rib are ideal here. The natural fat content of the meat will ensure that the patty does not become too dry. Veal (neck) is suitable and is milder and less fatty than beef. Beef and veal patties will be juiciest when cooked to medium, and definitely not to well done.

🐖 PORK

A patty made of fattier pork gets really juicy when it is fried a bit longer. That way it won't lose its flavor.

🐑 LAMB

If you like a particularly strong tasting meat for your patty, use lamb, ideally from the shoulder.

🐓 TURKEY & CHICKEN

Patties made of lean poultry meat can quickly dry out when frying. To prevent this, choose meat from the thigh instead of the breast, mix in some juicy pork, or ask the butcher to add some of the richer skin into the ground meat.

Important for all burgers: absolute freshness is essential when consuming ground meat!

A ROUND THING

There are two tricks for a particularly uniform and round patty:

1. The easiest way is with a burger press, available online for around $10.

2. If you're making the patty by hand, briefly knead the ground meat with wet hands, then bring it into a round, flat shape.

So that the patty doesn't turn into a meatball, press down in the middle of the raw patty with the back of a spoon to create an indent.

Let the patty cool for at least 1 hour before frying, so that the fat in the meat can harden somewhat, which gives the patty a firmer structure.

SO THAT NOTHING BURNS

The recipes in this book are intended for the indoor kitchen in that the patties are mainly prepared in the pan and oven. But any patty would be equally at home on a barbecue grill. For patties of poultry, fish, or seafood one should strengthen the patty's consistency with an egg and bread crumbs, or it might otherwise fall through the grill's grate. Burgers like it hot. They belong on a really hot grill or in a hot frying pan! And leave them be: flip them once or twice, that's enough. Keep it simple!

THE ASSISTANT—THE BUN

Put a lid on it for a perfect burger! On the following pages you will find recipes for great bun choices for your burger. You might even find a new favorite! For quicker prep, you can of course also fall back on a store-bought bun. Buns and rolls should be toasted slightly before serving so that they'll absorb less moisture and get an extra kick of flavor. Toast them either in the toaster, in a pan at medium heat, or on the grill.

READY, SET, BURGER!

Now that you are equipped with the most important tips and tricks to a good, tasty burger, you can let your imagination run wild with the fun ideas and suggestions in these recipes. Move in the right direction and give your burger that personal touch.

Blintzes

INGREDIENTS

1 ¾ CUPS MILK
1 TBSP FRESH YEAST
1 ⅓ CUPS PLAIN FLOUR
1 PINCH OF SALT
2 EGG YOLKS
2 EGG WHITES
3 TBSP HEAVY CREAM
CLARIFIED BUTTER FOR FRYING

PREPARATION

❶ Warm 1 ⅓ cups of milk in a pot. ❷ Dissolve the yeast in the warm milk, add ⅓ cup flour and mix into a dough. Let it sit for 15 minutes. ❸ Add the remaining flour, the remaining milk, salt, and egg yolks, and knead everything into a smooth dough. Let it sit for another 20 minutes. ❹ Whisk the egg whites and cream separately and add them into the dough alternately. ❺ Heat the clarified butter in a frying pan and turn the blintzes on both sides until golden brown.

Brioche Buns

MAKES APPROXIMATELY 4 BUNS

INGREDIENTS

2 TSP FRESH YEAST
4 TSP WATER
1 ⅓ CUPS FLOUR
3 OZ BUTTER
1 EGG
1 PINCH OF SALT
1 EGG FOR BRUSHING

PREPARATION

❶ Dissolve the yeast in 4 teaspoons of lukewarm water. Add half the flour to make a starter dough and let it sit for 1 hour. ❷ Mix the butter, now soft, in with the remaining ingredients, knead into a smooth dough, and then let it sit for another 30 minutes. ❸ Line a baking sheet with parchment paper. ❹ Divide the dough into four equally sized dough balls, lay them out on the sheet and let sit for another 30 minutes. ❺ Meanwhile, preheat the oven to 400°F. ❻ Brush the brioche buns with egg yolk and bake in the hot oven for 15–20 minutes.

Burger Buns

MAKES APPROXIMATELY 4 BUNS

INGREDIENTS

2 TSP FRESH YEAST
½ CUP WATER
1 CUP PLAIN FLOUR
1 EGG
1 ½ TSP SALT
1 TSP SUGAR
1 TBSP SOFT BUTTER
4 TSP SOURED MILK
BUTTER FOR BRUSHING

PREPARATION

❶ Crumble the yeast into the flour, add the remaining ingredients and ½ cup of water, knead well in a food processor, and let it rise for 1 hour. ❷ Divide the dough into four equal pieces, flatten them, and let rise for 30 minutes under foil or a kitchen towel. ❸ At the same time, line a baking sheet with parchment paper and preheat the oven to 350°F. ❹ Place the rolls onto the baking tray and bake in the hot oven for 15-20 minutes. ❺ Melt some butter, brush a coat onto the still-hot buns, and allow them to cool.

Curry-Chili Buns

MAKES 4–6 BUNS

INGREDIENTS

2 TSP FRESH YEAST
1 CUP FLOUR
½ CUP WATER
2 TBSP OLIVE OIL
½ TSP SALT
½ TSP INDIAN CURRY POWDER
1 PINCH CHILI POWDER
1 PINCH RED THAI CURRY PASTE

PREPARATION

❶ Dissolve the yeast in lukewarm water. Add half the flour to make a smooth dough. Let it rise for 1 hour. ❷ Add the remaining ingredients and knead well. ❸ Line a baking sheet with parchment paper. ❹ Make four to six equal dough balls, put them on the sheet, and let them sit again for 1 hour. ❺ Preheat the oven to 400°F. ❻ Bake the buns in the hot oven for about 10 minutes.

Fruity Bread Rolls

MAKES ABOUT 4 ROLLS

INGREDIENTS

2 TSP FRESH YEAST
1 ½ TBSP WATER
1 ⅓ CUP PLAIN FLOUR
3 OZ SOFT BUTTER
1 EGG
1 PINCH OF SALT
½ TSP VANILLA SUGAR
JUICE AND ZEST OF ½ SMALL LEMON
ZEST OF ½ ORANGE
1 EGG FOR BRUSHING

PREPARATION

❶ Dissolve the yeast in the lukewarm water. Add half the flour to make a smooth dough. Let it rise for 1 hour. ❷ Add the rest of the ingredients, one at a time, kneading well, and then let the dough rise for 1 hour. ❸ Line a baking tray with parchment paper. ❹ Divide the dough into four equal dough balls, distribute them on the tray, and let them sit again for 30 minutes. ❺ Preheat the oven to 450°F. ❻ Brush the rolls with egg yolk and bake in the hot oven for about 12 minutes.

Spiced Buns

INGREDIENTS

2 TSP FRESH YEAST
4 TBSP WATER
2 CUPS FLOUR
4 TBSP BUTTER
¼ TSP GROUND CUMIN
¼ TSP GROUND CORIANDER
½ TSP CHOPPED ROSEMARY
½ TSP CHOPPED THYME
1 PINCH BLACK PEPPER
OLIVE OIL FOR BRUSHING
SESAME SEEDS FOR SPRINKLING

PREPARATION

❶ Dissolve the yeast in 2 tablespoons of lukewarm water. Stir in the flour to make the dough and let it rise for about 1 hour. ❷ Add the remaining flour, softened butter, 2 tablespoons of water, and then the spices. Knead to a smooth dough and let it rise again for 1 more hour. ❸ Line a baking tray with parchment paper. ❹ Form the dough into four equally large dough balls, put on the baking tray, and let rise for 1 hour. ❺ Preheat the oven to 400°F. ❻ Brush the buns with olive oil and sprinkle with the sesame seeds, carefully slice into the top crosswise, and bake in the hot oven for 15 minutes.

Olive-Focaccia

MAKES APPROXIMATELY 4 PIECES

INGREDIENTS

2 CUPS FLOUR
1 TBSP FRESH YEAST
½ CUP WATER
½ TSP SALT
1 TBSP OLIVE OIL
1 TBSP BLACK OLIVES, FINELY CHOPPED
OLIVE OIL FOR BRUSHING
COARSE SEA SALT FOR SPRINKLING

PREPARATION

❶ Add the flour into a bowl and make a hollow dent in the middle. Crumble the yeast into it. ❷ Make the starter dough with about 2 tablespoons of lukewarm water, mix gently, and let it rise. ❸ Add ½ cup of lukewarm water, salt, oil, and olives, then knead to a smooth dough. ❹ Let the dough rise in the fridge for 2 hours. ❺ Line a baking sheet with parchment paper. ❻ Shape the dough into four equal dough balls, set out on the sheet, brush with olive oil, sprinkle with coarse sea salt, and let it sit again for 30 minutes. ❼ Preheat the oven to 400°F. ❽ Bake the focaccia in the hot oven for 15 minutes.

Squid Ink Buns

MAKES APPROXIMATELY 4 BUNS

INGREDIENTS

2 CUPS FLOUR
½ CUPS WATER
1 TBSP FRESH YEAST
½ TSP SALT
1 EGG YOLK
1 TSP OLIVE OIL
1 TSP SQUID INK
OLIVE OIL FOR BRUSHING

PREPARATION

❶ Add the flour into a bowl and make a hollow dent in the middle. Crumble the yeast into it. ❷ Make a starter dough with about 2 tablespoons of lukewarm water, mix carefully and let it rise. ❸ Add the remaining ingredients, ⅓ cup lukewarm water, and knead everything into a smooth dough. ❹ Let the dough cool in the fridge for 2 hours. ❺ Line a baking sheet with parchment paper. ❻ Shape the dough into four equally large dough balls, set out on the sheet, brush with olive oil and let it sit again for 30 minutes. ❼ Preheat the oven to 400°F. ❽ Bake the buns in the hot oven for about 15 minutes.

Sesame Buns

INGREDIENTS

¼ CUP MILK
¼ CUP WATER
4 TSP FRESH YEAST
2 CUPS FLOUR
½ TSP SALT
1 EGG YOLK
1 TSP TOASTED SESAME OIL
½ TSP SESAME PASTE
BUTTER FOR BRUSHING
SESAME SEEDS FOR SPRINKLING

PREPARATION

❶ Warm the milk, stir in the lukewarm water, and dissolve the yeast in it. ❷ Make a smooth starter dough by adding half the flour and let it rise for 1 hour. ❸ Mix in the remaining ingredients knead the dough, and let it sit for another 30 minutes. ❹ Line a baking sheet with parchment paper. ❺ Form four equal dough balls on the sheet and again let it rise for 30 minutes. ❻ Preheat the oven to 400°F. ❼ Melt butter and brush it onto the buns, sprinkle them with the sesame seeds, and bake in the hot oven about 25 minutes.

Tomato Buns

MAKES 4 BUNS

INGREDIENTS

⅓ CUP MILK
4 TSP FRESH YEAST
1 ½ CUPS FLOUR
1 SMALL ONION
4 TBSP SUN-DRIED TOMATOES
2 BASIL LEAVES
5 TSP OIL OF MARINATED TOMATOES
5 TSP OLIVE OIL
1 EGG YOLK
¼ TSP SALT
½ CUP SUGAR
1 PINCH TOMATO PASTE
OLIVE OIL FOR FRYING
COARSE SEA SALT FOR SPRINKLING

PREPARATION

❶ Warm the milk and dissolve the yeast in it. ❷ Add half the flour into the mix, knead gently, and leave it in the fridge for 2 hours. ❸ Peel and finely dice the onion, sauté in olive oil. ❹ Finely dice the tomatoes. ❺ Wash the basil leaves, shake dry, and cut into fine strips. ❻ Work the onions, tomato, basil, and remaining ingredients into the dough. ❼ Line a baking sheet with parchment paper. ❽ Shape four equal dough balls and arrange them on the sheet. Let them sit for another 30 minutes. ❾ Preheat the oven to 400°F. ❿ Brush the tomato buns with water, sprinkle with coarse salt, and bake them for about 15 minutes in the hot oven.

Whole Wheat Buns

MAKES ABOUT 4–6 BUNS

INGREDIENTS: STARTER DOUGH

2 ½ TBSP FLAXSEED
2 ½ TBSP OATMEAL
2 ½ TBSP SUNFLOWER SEEDS
2 ½ TBSP SESAME SEEDS
¼ CUP RYE WHOLE MEAL FLOUR
1 PINCH OF SALT
⅓ CUP WATER

INGREDIENTS: MAIN DOUGH

THE STARTER DOUGH
2 CUPS WHOLE WHEAT FLOUR
2 TBSP BUTTER
1 TBSP FRESH YEAST
⅓ CUP WATER
½ TSP SALT
½ TSP SUGAR
1 EGG YOLK
RAW GRAINS FOR SPRINKLING

PREPARATION

❶ Add all ingredients for the starter dough into a bowl, add ⅓ cup of water, and mix everything well. Let the starter dough rise in the refrigerator for 12 hours. ❷ Mix flour, butter, yeast, as well as ⅓ cup water into it, and add the salt, sugar, and egg yolk. Mix everything well and let it rise again for 12 hours in the refrigerator. ❸ Line a baking sheet with parchment paper. ❹ Form the dough into four to six equal dough balls and place on the tray. Brush with water, sprinkle on grains, and let them sit for 30 more minutes. ❺ Preheat the oven to 375°F. ❻ Bake the buns for about 20 minutes in the hot oven.

Walnut Buns

INGREDIENTS

½ CUP CHOPPED WALNUTS
½ CUP MILK
1 ½ TBSP YEAST
¾ CUP PLAIN FLOUR
¾ CUP RYE FLOUR
¼ CUP WHOLE WHEAT FLOUR
1 TSP SALT
1 PINCH OF SUGAR

PREPARATION

❶ Roast the walnuts in an ungreased nonstick frying pan.
❷ Warm the milk and dissolve the yeast in it. ❸ Add the remaining ingredients to the yeasty milk, knead everything to a smooth dough, and let it sit for 1 hour. ❹ Line a baking sheet with parchment paper. ❺ Form the dough into four equal dough balls, lay them out on the tray, and again let them sit for 30 minutes. ❻ Preheat the oven to 425°F. ❼ Bake the buns in the hot oven for about 15 minutes.

Aioli

Ingredients

4 cloves of garlic / 1 egg yolk / 1 cup olive oil / 1 splash lemon juice / Salt
and freshly ground black pepper

Preparation

1 | Finely chop the garlic. **2** | In a small bowl, stir egg yolk, garlic, salt and pepper into a creamy mix. **3** | Gradually stir in the olive oil to make a homogeneous mixture. **4** | Season with lemon juice, salt, and pepper to taste.

Barbecue Sauce

ingredients

4 cloves of garlic

3 medium-sized onions

1 red chili pepper

2 Tbsp olive oil

1 shot of strong espresso (5 *tsp*)

2 Tbsp honey

1 Tbsp soy sauce

1 Tbsp Worcestershire sauce

1 Tbsp spicy rose pepper powder

3 Tbsp tomato ketchup

1 Tbsp Dijon mustard

1 Tbsp brandy vinegar

Salt and freshly ground black pepper

Preparation

Finely chop the garlic cloves and onions. Then, finely chop the chili pepper. Fry together in some olive oil. Deglaze with the espresso, allow it to cool, then add the remaining ingredients and let marinate in the fridge overnight.

 To enhance the typically smoky taste of the BBQ sauce, simply add liquid smoke in a hickory or mesquite flavor.

Caesar Dressing

Preparation:

| 1 |

Peel and finely chop the garlic.

| 2 |

Mix garlic,
parmesan,
Worcestershire sauce,
egg,
mustard and lemon juice
in a food processor.

| 3 |

Slowly add the
olive oil in a thin
stream and blend to
a smooth emulsion.

| 4 |

Finally, season the
dressing with salt
and pepper to taste.

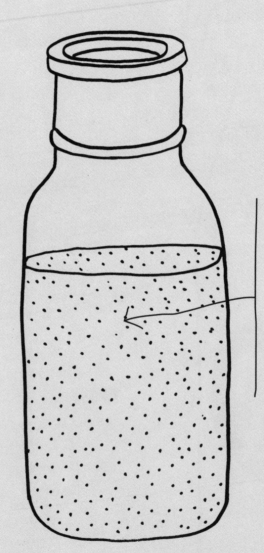

Ingredients:

1 garlic clove

2 Tbsp freshly grated parmesan
cheese

1 Tbsp Worcestershire sauce

1 egg

1 tsp mustard

2 Tbsp lemon juice

1 cup olive oil

Salt and freshly ground
black pepper

INGREDIENTS

3 Tbsp ketchup

½ tsp spicy mustard

1 cup mayonnaise (page 28)

1 Tbsp Worcestershire sauce

1 Tsp brandy

1 Tsp sherry

Salt and cayenne pepper

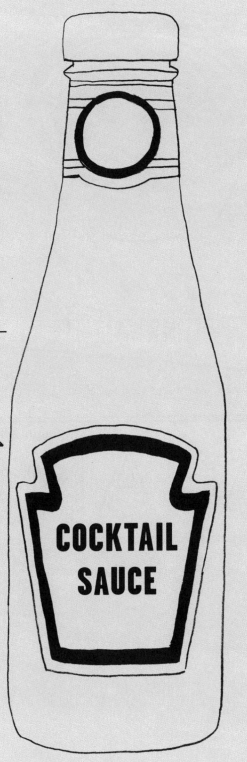

COCKTAIL SAUCE

PREPARATION

1 | Gently mix ketchup, mustard, mayonnaise, Worcestershire sauce, brandy, and sherry.

2 | Season with salt and cayenne pepper to taste.

↕

2 vine-ripe tomatoes / 1 shallot / 2 avocados / 2 tsp olive oil / juice of 1 lime / 1 dash Tabasco / salt

GUACAMOLE

1 | Dip the vine-ripe tomatoes for 20 seconds into boiling water, then immediately into ice water. Peel and core, then cut into cubes. **2** | Peel and finely dice the shallot. **3** | Cut the avocados in half, remove the pit, and remove the pulp with a spoon. Mash with a fork. **4** | Add in tomatoes, shallot, olive oil, and lime juice, and season to taste with salt and Tabasco.

↕

PREPARATION

Hollandaise

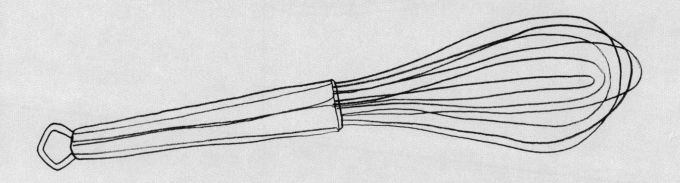

Ingredients

1 egg

1 Tbsp white wine vinegar

1 Tbsp dry white wine

⅓ cup of clarified butter

Juice of ½ lemon

Salt and freshly ground
black pepper

Preparation

1 | Whisk the egg with vinegar, white wine, and 1 Tbsp water in a bowl over a water bath until foamy.

2 | Add the warm butter very slowly, in a thin stream while constantly whisking, creating a homogeneous cream.

3 | Season to taste with lemon juice, salt, and pepper.

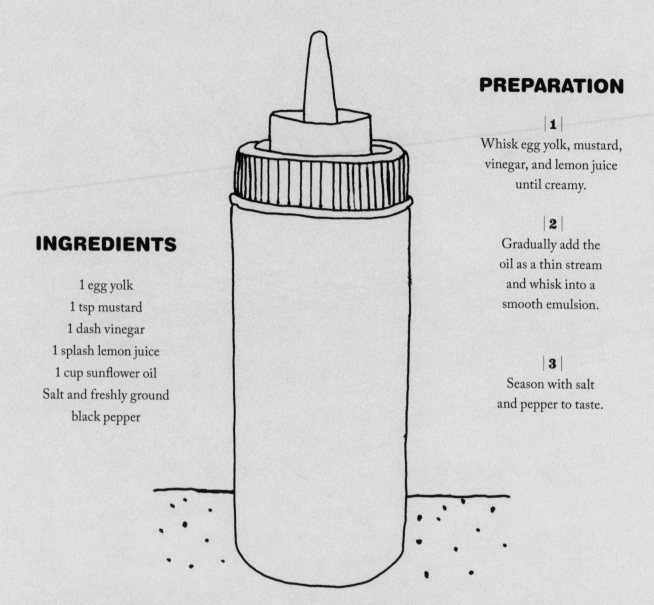

PREPARATION

| 1 |

Whisk egg yolk, mustard,
vinegar, and lemon juice
until creamy.

| 2 |

Gradually add the
oil as a thin stream
and whisk into a
smooth emulsion.

| 3 |

Season with salt
and pepper to taste.

INGREDIENTS

1 egg yolk
1 tsp mustard
1 dash vinegar
1 splash lemon juice
1 cup sunflower oil
Salt and freshly ground
black pepper

MAYONNAISE

PESTO

INGREDIENTS 4 bunches of basil / ½ cup pine nuts / 2 cloves garlic / ½ cup parmesan / ½ cup olive oil / 1 tsp sea salt   **PREPARATION** **1** | Wash the basil, shake dry, and pluck the leaves from the stems. **2** | Toast the pine nuts in an ungreased pan. **3** | Peel and chop the garlic. **4** | Grate the parmesan cheese. **5** | Crush garlic and sea salt in a large mortar. **6** | Add and crush the pine nuts. **7** | Add and crush the basil leaves. **8** | Mix in the grated cheese. **9** | Transfer to a bowl and slowly stir in oil, until a smooth paste is formed.

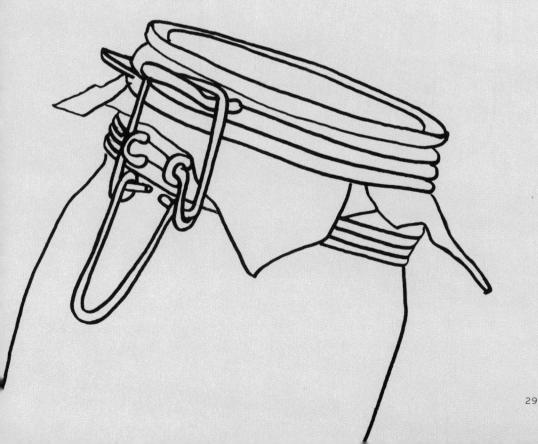

INGREDIENTS

3 cups fresh plums or prunes / 2 red onions / 1 Tbsp sunflower oil / 1 Tbsp ginger / juice and zest of 1 orange / ½ cup dark balsamic vinegar / 4 Tbsp cane sugar / 1 pinch ground allspice / 1 pinch ground coriander / 1 pinch mustard powder / 1 pinch cayenne pepper / salt

PREPARATION

1 | Wash, core, and quarter fresh plums or prunes. **2** | Finely dice the onions and sauté in oil in a pot until translucent. **3** | Finely grate the ginger into the mix. **4** | Add the other ingredients into the saucepan and cook everything on low heat for 45 minutes until thickened. **5** | Pour hot chutney into jars.

INGREDIENTS ➤ 2 hard-boiled eggs / ½ clove of garlic / 1 shallot / 1 green bell pepper / a handful of flat-leaf parsley / 1 small pickle / 2 anchovy fillets / 1 teaspoon capers / 10 basil leaves / 1 cup olive oil / 2 Tbsp white wine vinegar / Salt and freshly ground black pepper

SALSA VERDE

PREPARATION ➤ **1** │ Peel and coarsely chop the garlic and shallots. **2** │ Wash and coarsely chop the green pepper. **3** │ Wash the parsley, shake dry, and pluck the leaves from the stems. **4** │ Boil and peel the eggs. **5** │ Cut the pickle into slices. **6** │ In a blender, mix the eggs, garlic, shallot, bell pepper, parsley, pickle, anchovies, capers, and basil with the oil and vinegar into a creamy consistency. **7** │ Spice the salsa verde with salt and pepper to taste.

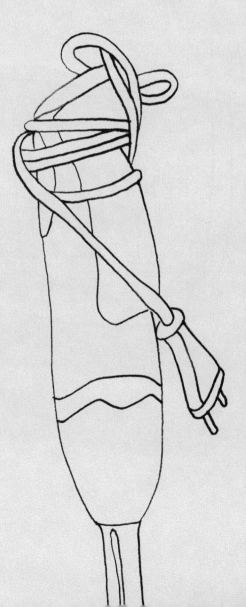

PREPARATION

| 1 |

Hard boil the eggs in
some water.

| 2 |

Drain the capers and
chop finely.

| 3 |

Wash the herbs and
shake dry.

| 4 |

Cut the chives finely.
Chop parsley, garden
chervil, and tarragon.

| 5 |

Peel the eggs and
mash the yolks
in a bowl.

| 6 |

Pour the olive oil
in a thin stream,
constantly stirring
to obtain a homogeneous
mixture.

| 7 |

Stir in the chopped herbs
and capers.

| 8 |

Season the tartar sauce
with lemon juice, salt, and
pepper to taste.

INGREDIENTS

2 eggs

1 Tbsp capers

½ bunch chives

2 Tbsp parsley

5 branches of chervil

1 branch of tarragon

⅔ cup olive oil

Juice of ½ lemon

Salt

Fresh ground black pepper

OW TO US THIS BOOK

LEGEND

S *speedy preparation*   **M** *medium preparation*   **L** *long preparation*

(4) 🍴 *Recipe for a specified number of people*

....

- PIG
- BEEF
- VEAL
- LAMB
- CHICKEN
- DUCK
- SEAFOOD
- FISH
- VEGETARIAN
- SWEET

- BREAD ROLLS
- SAUCE
- SALAD
- CHEESE
- VEGETABLES
- FRUIT
- HERBS
- NUTS
- ICE CREAM
- CHOCOLATE

....

POWER TO THE PEOPLE | Decide for yourself which elements of the burger recipes you want to make first *(see Burger with Handkäse and Music, page 41)*. The recipes are arranged to correspond to the layers of the burgers in the layouts, not to the absolute best chronological order. Find the correct order of steps for the combination-burgers *(for example, Pretzel Burger, page 36/37)* by using the specific numbers. In general, follow this motto: read first, then think, then do!

BURGER NAVIGATOR

PRETZEL BURGER ground pork – onion – pickle – liverwurst → 36

LAY THEE DOWN Weisswurst – cabbage – pickles – radish – bacon → 39

BURGER WITH HANDKÄSE AND MUSIC Handkäse (sour milk cheese) – onion – apple – cumin → 41

HOP TO IT apple – sauerkraut – blood sausage – onion → 42

THE FALSE HARE ground pork – onion – apple → 44

JÄGER BURGER veal – shallot – mushroom → 46

KÖNIGSBERGER red beets – ground beef/veal – capers – anchovies → 48

CAPITAL CITY ground veal – veal liver – onion – apple → 50

BERLIN AIR doughnuts – sparkling wine – raspberry – mint → 53

SKYSCRAPER boiled beef – potato – cheese – herbs – cucumber – egg → 54

HEALTH CITY cottage cheese – cucumber – radish – sprouts – spelt → 56

BOY, COME HOME SOON smoked pork – potato – pickled herring – red beet – onion – egg → 58

BISMARCK-BURGER Bismarck (pickled) herring – egg – pickle – onion → 60

DANNEBROG whole grain rye bread – kippers – onion – radish – egg → 63

THE MOUNTAIN CALLS hash browns – ground beef – dried beef – Gruyère – bacon → 64

CORDON BLEU BURGER veal – asparagus – ham – Emmentaler or Jarlsberg cheese → 66

BROTHER JAKOB scallops – spinach – peas – carrots → 69

PARIS PARIS ground chicken – truffle – foie gras – plum → 71

CAMEMBURGER camembert – cranberry – cress → 72

GO BLUES ground beef – blue cheese – bacon – fig mustard → 75

TARTARE HALF BAKED beef tenderloin – wild herb salad – cucumber – capers – onion → 76

À LA NIÇOISE ground veal – tuna – egg – onion – anchovies → 79

BE HUNGRY—BE RICH lobster – Serrano ham – seaweed – lime – avocado → 80

PEACH, WIND, & CHOCOLATE cream puffs – peach – chocolate – vanilla ice cream → 83

SUNNY SIDE UP ground beef – egg – truffle – Madeira wine → 85

CAPRESE—GEDDIT? ground beef – mozzarella – tomato – arugula → 86

THE ITALIAN JOB pastrami – ham – burrata – arugula – tomato → 88

MUY CALIENTE beef – chorizo – jalapeño – arugula – tomato → 90

PRAWNY shrimp – fennel – radicchio – olive → 93

THE OLD GREEK ground lamb – feta – yogurt – white cabbage – bell pepper → 94

TSAR NIKOLAJ blintzes – salmon – smoked salmon – caviar → 96

BREAKFAST @ TIFFANY'S bratwurst – eggs – bacon – cheese – tomato → 98

CREAM AND CHEESE beef – cheese – jalapeños – radicchio – cheddar → 101

THE BIG APPLE duck breast – celery – walnut – apple – pineapple → 103

CLUB BURGER chicken breast – bacon – tomato – cucumber → 104

CAESAR BURGER turkey breast – Romaine lettuce – parmesan – anchovy → 106

BENEDICT BURGER veal – ham – egg – bacon – spinach → 109

HEY COWBOY ground beef – cheddar – bacon – pickles – tomato → 111

FARMER'S LUNCH ground beef – sweet potato – bacon – BBQ sauce → 112

RED HOT CHILI BURGER ground beef – beans – bacon – papaya – chili → 114

SMOKER'S EMPIRE beef – onion – pepper – pickles – bacon → 116

GO YELLOW ground chicken – orange – curry – lime → 118

CRAB ME GOOD crab – bok choy – avocado – mango → 120

AVOTUNA BURGER tuna – wild herb salad – avocado → 123

THE FAST (FOOD) SAMURAI tofu – bean sprouts – shiitake mushrooms – ginger → 124

BIG IN JAPAN ground beef – bok choy – oyster mushrooms – shiso cress → 126

BOLLYWOOD ground chicken – yogurt – mango – ginger – coconut → 128

ORIENT EXPRESS chickpeas – carrot – yogurt – onion – cucumber → 130

1001 NIGHTS lamb – chickpea – avocado – date → 133

ARE YOU CRAZY? waffle – pineapple – coconut – mint → 134

GROUND PORK

①

Mix the ground meat with ½ teaspoon salt and ¼ teaspoon pepper and make four equally large patties (approx. ½ in. thick). Make a dent in the middle with a spoon and cool in the fridge for approximately 1 hour.

⑧

Wash the lettuce leaves and shake dry.

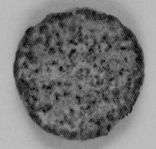

⑦

Preheat the oven to 350°F . Give the patties a quick fry in clarified butter on both sides and bake in the hot oven for about 10 minutes.

LIVERWURST

INGREDIENTS — *1 lb. ground pork | ⅓ lb. homemade liver sausage | 1 Tbsp hot mustard | 1 Tbsp barbecue sauce (page 23) | 2 medium-sized onions | 2 pickles | 4 radishes | 4 lettuce leaves | 4 large pretzel rolls | Salt and freshly ground black pepper | Clarified butter for frying*

②

Blend liver sausage, mustard, and barbecue sauce with a fork into a creamy mix.

⑨ **STACKING**

Cut the rolls in half, lightly toast the insides, and place lettuce on the bottom piece. Spread the liver sausage, add the patty, garnish with caramelized onions, pickles, and radish and add the top to complete it.

ONION

PICKLES

③ — ⑥

Drain the pickles and cut into slices. | Clean, dry, and slice the radishes. | Peel the onions, cut into strips, and sauté in 1 Tbsp clarified butter until caramelized.

PRETZEL BURGER

LAY THEE DOWN

🐷 ④ 🍴 S̲

¼ **SMALL CABBAGE**

1 SMALL ONION

1 TBSP WHITE WINE VINEGAR

4 TSP SUNFLOWER OIL

1 PINCH OF SUGAR

3 PAIRS WEISSWURST (ABOUT 1 LB)

½ CUP RADISHES

8 SLICES OF BACON

2 LARGE PICKLES

4 NICE ICEBERG LETTUCE LEAVES

4 TBSP SWEET MUSTARD

4 PRETZEL ROLLS

3 ½ TBSP MAYONNAISE (PAGE 28)

¼ TSP CUMIN POWDER

Salt and freshly ground black pepper

1 / Clean the cabbage and cut into fine strips. **2** / Peel the onion, finely dice, and add to the cabbage. **3** / Marinate the cabbage with oil and 2 TSP vinegar, mix vigorously and season to taste with salt, pepper, and a pinch of sugar. **4** / Warm up the Weisswurst in hot, but not boiling salted water for 10 minutes, then peel and cut in half lengthwise. **5** / Wash the radish, cut into thin slices, then marinate with salt and the remaining white vinegar. **6** / Fry the bacon to crispy in a pan. **7** / Drain the pickles and slice diagonally. **8** / Wash the lettuce leaves and shake dry. **9** / Halve the buns and lightly toast the insides. **10** / Mix the mayonnaise with cumin powder spread on the undersides. **11** / Add the lettuce leaves and cucumber slices. Spread the cabbage evenly and lay down three Weisswurst halves. **12** / Brush with mustard, add the radish, top with bacon slices, and finish with the lids. 👉

BURGER
WITH HANDKÄSE AND MUSIC

HANDKASE / ONION / APPLE / CUMIN

4

S

BURGER BUNS   Prepare the burger buns per the recipe on page 12. Sprinkle with cumin before baking.

HANDKASE   Peel the onions, cut into small cubes and blanch briefly. Cut the cheese into slices. Stir the vinegar, apple cider, and oil into a marinade. Add the onion and 1 TSP cumin, then season with salt and pepper to taste. Marinate the cheese for 1 day in the fridge.

APPLE SLICES   Fry the apple slices in 1 TBSP clarified butter until translucent.

SALAD   Wash the lettuce leaves and shake dry.

CUMIN MAYONNAISE   Prepare the mayonnaise recipe on page 28. Mix the mayonnaise with ½ TSP cumin powder.

BURGER BUNS

INGREDIENTS

4 burger buns (recipe on page 12)

2 medium-sized onions

1 ⅓ lbs. of sour milk cheese (Handkäse)

4 TBSP white wine vinegar

4 TBSP cider

4 TBSP sunflower oil

1 TSP cumin

8 thin slices of apple

Clarified butter for frying

8 lettuce heart leaves

½ cup mayonnaise (page 28)

½ TBSP cumin powder

½ bunch chives

Salt and freshly ground black pepper

STACKING   Halve the rolls, lightly toast the insides. Spread the mayonnaise on the halves. Place two lettuce leaves, then a slice of apple on the bottom halves of the buns. Strain the marinated cheese and spread evenly. Finely cut the chives, sprinkle, cover with another slice of apple, and finish with the bread's lid.

10 Cut the rolls in half and lightly toast the insides.

8 Wash the lettuce leaves and shake dry.

3 + **4** Peel the onions and cut into strips. | Cook onions in some clarified butter in a pan, pour on Riesling, and cook down.

9 Stir the mustard into the mayonnaise.

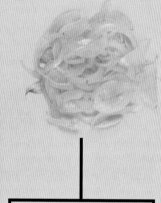

ONION

INGREDIENTS — *4 TBSP canned sauerkraut | 1 TBSP white wine vinegar | 3 TBSP sunflower oil | 2 medium-sized onions | 2 TBSP Riesling | 2 small apples (approx. 1 cup) | 1 TBSP sugar | 12 slices blood sausage (approximately ⅔ in. thick) | 4 lettuce leaves | 4 burger buns (page 12) | ¼ cup mayonnaise (page 28) | 1 TBSP spicy mustard | Salt and fresh ground black pepper | Clarified butter for frying | Flour for dusting*

HOP TO IT

  4 ΨΙ S

APPLE

❶ + ❷

Start with the Sauerkraut in a small bowl. | Mix a marinade of the white wine vinegar and oil, season with salt and pepper to taste, and simmer the sauerkraut for 1 hour in it.

❺ + ❻

Peel and core, then chop up the apples. | Bring the apple pieces with sugar and ¼ cup of water in a saucepan to a boil. Cook covered to a puree.

SAUERKRAUT

❼

Sprinkle the blood sausage with flour, if necessary, and sear in clarified butter for 3 minutes on both sides over medium heat until golden-brown.

BLOOD SAUSAGE

⓫ STACKING

Coat the bottom halves of the buns with mayonnaise. Place the salad leaves and cover with the onion. Drain the sauerkraut and distribute onto the onion. Then layer with the blood sausage, coat with 1 TBSP applesauce, and complete with the cover.

THE FALSE HARE

5 MEDIUM-SIZED ONIONS

1 APPLE

2 TBSP HONEY

2 TBSP DARK BALSAMIC VINEGAR

1/4 CUP APPLE JUICE

1 SPLASH LEMON JUICE

1 1/3 LB FRESH GROUND PORK

8 CRISP ICEBERG LETTUCE LEAVES

4 WHOLE WHEAT BUNS {PAGE 20}

SALT AND FRESHLY GROUND BLACK PEPPER

CLARIFIED BUTTER FOR FRYING

BUTTER FOR BRUSHING

1 / Peel the onions and cut into rings. **2** / Peel the apple and grate coarsely with the kitchen grater. **3** / Sauté three quarters of the onions in clarified butter until golden brown. **4** / Add the apple along with balsamic vinegar, honey, and apple juice for a quick simmer. Add a little lemon juice to taste. **5** / Form the ground pork into four equal patties. Preheat the oven to 350°F. Give the patties a quick fry in clarified butter on both sides and bake in the hot oven for about 10 minutes. **6** / Wash the salad leaves and shake dry. **7** / Halve the buns, lightly toast the insides, allow to cool, and coat all sides with butter. **8** / Lay down salad leaves, evenly put sautéed onions on the bottom halves, place the patties on top, garnish with raw onion rings, and finish with the bread tops.

JÄGER BURGER

VEAL / SHALLOT / MUSHROOM

INGREDIENTS — *4 shallots | 2 TBSP red wine | ½ cup mayonnaise (page 28) | 1 pinch paprika powder | 8 large mushrooms | 1 TBSP tomato paste | 1 TSP flour | 1 cup heavy cream | 1 TBSP red wine vinegar | 1⅓ lb. veal tenderloins, kitchen ready | 4 leaves of red leaf lettuce | 4 walnut buns (page 21) | 2 onions | Salt and freshly ground black pepper | Clarified butter for frying | Flour for dusting | Oil for deep frying*

1 / Peel the shallots, put two aside, then cut the rest into strips. Sauté strips in clarified butter until golden brown. Deglaze with the red wine and cook down some.

2 / After cooling the shallots, mix in the mayonnaise and salt, pepper, and paprika to taste.

3 / Cut the remaining shallots and six of the mushrooms into cubes and sauté in clarified butter.

4 / Add the tomato paste, stir, and sprinkle on flour. Cook up quickly to roast and then add cream. Simmer down and season with salt and pepper to taste.

5 / Cut the remaining raw mushrooms into thin slices and marinate with a little vinegar and salt.

6 / Cut the veal tenderloins into eight equal slices, flatten lightly with a meat mallet, season with salt and pepper and cook with 1 TBSP clarified butter for 3 minutes on both sides over medium heat.

7 / Wash the lettuce leaves and shake dry.

8 / Peel the onions and cut into rings, sprinkle with flour, and fry until golden in hot oil at 325°F. Drain onto paper towels and season with salt.

9 / Halve the burger buns, lightly toast the insides, and spread shallot-mayonnaise. Layer the salad leaves and the first four veal cutlets on the bottom halves.

10 / Spread half of the mushroom sauce on the cutlets. Place the other four cutlets on top and cover with the remaining mushroom sauce.

11 / Garnish with the marinated mushroom slices and the fried onions and finish with the lids.

KÖNIGS-BERGER

  S

RED
BEETS →

1 + 2

Thinly slice the red beets. | Mix a marinade from red wine vinegar and sunflower oil. Season with salt, pepper, and cumin powder to taste and marinate the beets in it overnight.

8 — 10

Chop the remaining capers into the mayonnaise and mix. | Wash the lettuce leaves and shake dry. | Halve the rolls, lightly toast the insides, and spread with the mayonnaise.

GROUND BEEF / GROUND VEAL

3 + 4

Peel the onion and finely dice. | Finely chop the capers.

5

Season the ground meat with the onions, 1 TBSP chopped capers, parsley, marjoram, ½ TSP salt, and ¼ TSP pepper. Knead and form four equal patties (approx. ½ in. thick) and refrigerate for 1 hour.

CAPERS

TIP FOR CAPER FANS

Use some fried capers as a topping for the anchovies. For this, pat dry the capers on kitchen paper towels. Deep fry the capers in 350°F hot vegetable oil for about 15 seconds, then drip dry them again on the paper towels. Salt lightly.

ANCHOVIES

6 + 7

Cover the bottom of a large pot with water, add a bay leaf, peppercorns, clove, and boil. | Place the patties on a steam tray in the pot, close the lid, and cook the patty in the vapors for about 10 minutes.

⑪ STACKING

Place a salad leaf on each of the bottoms of the buns, then add the patty. Take the red beets from the marinade, strain, and layer over the patties. Finish with the anchovies and the bread's lids.

INGREDIENTS — *2 cooked red beets | 2 TSP red wine vinegar | 2 TSBP sunflower oil | 1 pinch of cumin powder | 1 medium-sized onion | 3 TBSP capers | ¾ lbs. ground beef | 1 lb. ground veal | 2 TBSP chopped parsley | 1 pinch of oregano powder | 1 bay leaf | 6 peppercorns | 1 clove | ½ cup mayonnaise (page 28) | 4 iceberg lettuce leaves | 4 burger buns (page 12) | 4 anchovy fillets | salt and freshly ground black pepper*

CAPITAL CITY

GROUND VEAL / VEAL LIVER / ONION / APPLE

4

M

BURGER BUNS   Prepare the burger buns from the recipe on page 18.

FRIED ONIONS   Peel the onions and cut into rings. Fry half of the onions in the 350°F hot vegetable oil, drain onto paper towels, and lightly season with salt.

CARAMELIZED APPLE SLICES   Peel apples, remove core, and slice eight even slices. Caramelize the sugar to a bright color in a pot, deglaze with the Calvados, let it cook down, and caramelize the apple slices in about 30 seconds.

VEAL LIVER   Slice the liver piece into four equally large cuts, coat in flour, and cook in 1 TBSP clarified butter at medium heat for 3 minutes.

BALSAMIC ONIONS   Cook the other half of the onion rings in some clarified butter until golden brown. Stir in the balsamic vinegar and simmer down.

PATTY   Mix the ground veal with ½ TSP salt and ¼ TSP pepper loosely and make four large patties (approx. 1/3 in. thick), then refrigerate for 1 hour. Shortly before stacking the burgers, heat some clarified butter in a frying pan and fry the burgers for 4 minutes on each side.

SALAD   Wash the lettuce leaves and shake dry.

MAYONNAISE   Prepare the mayonnaise recipe on page 28. Pick some parsley, blanche in boiling water, cool in ice water, strain, and mix into the mayonnaise.

BURGER BUNS

INGREDIENTS

4 sesame seed buns (page 18)

4 medium-sized onions

Vegetable oil for frying

1 large apple (such as Granny Smith)

1 TBSP sugar

2 TSP Calvados (apple brandy)

¾ lb. veal liver

4 TBSP flour

2 TSP balsamic vinegar

1 lb. ground veal

4 iceberg lettuce leaves

1 cup mayonnaise (page 28)

1 bunch flat-leaf parsley

Salt and freshly ground black pepper

Clarified butter for frying

STACKING   Halve buns, lightly toast the insides, and spread with parsley mayonnaise. Place the leaves of lettuce on the lower halves, then a patty. Spread balsamic onions, then a slice of apple, then the veal liver, then another slice of apple, and fried onions. Complete with the bun tops.

BERLIN AIR

4 BIG JELLY DOUGHNUTS (BERLINERS)
(ORDER AT THE BAKERY WITHOUT FILLING)
2 LEAVES OF GELATIN
2 EGGS
¼ CUP SUGAR
CORE OF 1 VANILLA BEAN
1 TBSP LEMON JUICE
¼ CUP CHAMPAGNE
JUICE OF 1 LIME
½ CUP SUGAR
1 BUNCH MINT
3 TBSP ALMOND FLOUR
50 RASPBERRIES
1 TBSP RASPBERRY BRANDY
1 TBSP POWDERED SUGAR
SALT

1 / Soak the gelatin in cold water. **2** / Separate the eggs, set aside the egg whites. **3** / Mix the egg yolks with sugar and vanilla, mix and whip until fluffy, then add the lemon juice at the end. **4** / Heat the sparkling wine, carefully ring the water out of the gelatin, dissolve in the champagne, and gradually stir in the yolks. **5** / Beat the egg whites with a pinch of salt until stiff and stir into the cooled cream, then refrigerate 2 hours. **6** / In a pot, bring ¼ cup of water with the lime juice and sugar to a boil, and leave to cool. **7** / Wash mint, shake dry, and pluck the leaves from the stems. **8** / Mix the sugar-lime-water with the mint and almond flour to a fine puree. **9** / Wash the raspberries carefully in a colander, pat dry, and marinate with powdered sugar and raspberry spirit. **10** / Cut the doughnut in half and use a pastry bag to pipe the egg mixture on both halfs. **11** / Add 12 raspberries per bun, garnish with mint pesto, and finish with the tops. 👉

SKYSCRAPER

2 SMALL CARROTS
2 STICKS PERENNIAL CELERY
2 ONIONS
1 BAY LEAF
4 ALLSPICE GRANULES
8 BLACK PEPPERCORNS
2 TBSP COARSE SALT
1 ⅓ LBS. VEAL RUMP
1 TBSP CORNFLOUR
2 POTATOES
2 EGGS
1½ CUPS MIXED HERBS
(PARSLEY, SORREL,
LEMON BALM, PIMPERNEL, DILL,
LOVAGE, BORAGE, WATERCRESS)
½ CUP SOUR CREAM
½ CUP CREAM CHEESE
1 TBSP MUSTARD / ½ TBSP HERB VINEGAR / 1 TBSP GRAPE SEED OIL
4 NICE LETTUCE LEAVES
4 BURGER BUNS (PAGE 12)
12 SLICES CUCUMBER
SALT AND FRESHLY GROUND BLACK PEPPER
CLARIFIED BUTTER FOR FRYING
OIL FOR DEEP FRYING

1 / Peel and dice carrots, celery, and onions, sauté in 1 TBSP clarified butter, and deglaze with approximately 2 quarts water. **2** / Add bay leaf, allspice, peppercorns, and coarse salt, stir, bring broth to a boil, put the rump in and cook over low heat for approximately 1½–2 hours until it is soft. **3** / Take out the meat, let cool, and cut thinly. **4** / Mix about ½ cup of broth with cornstarch and marinate the slices in it. **5** / Peel the potatoes, cut into thin strips, wash well, pat dry, and fry in 350°F hot oil until golden brown. Drain onto paper towels. **6** / Make hard boiled eggs in some water. **7** / Wash the herbs, shake dry, and pluck from stems. Set aside about ⅓ cup of the mixture. **8** / Puree the rest with sour cream and cream cheese in a mixer and season with mustard, salt, and pepper to taste. **9** / Marinate the set-aside herbs with oil and vinegar and season with salt and pepper. **10** / Peel the eggs and slice. **11** / Wash the lettuce leaves and shake dry. **12** / Cut the rolls in half, lightly toast the insides, and smear them with the green herb spread. **13** / Cover the bottoms with lettuce leaves, smear on more herb spread, place marinated veal slices on top. Layer cucumber, eggs, marinated herbs, fried potatoes, and finish with the bun's lids. 🍶

INGREDIENTS — *Mixed sprouts | 2 TBSP grape seed oil | 1 TBSP herb vinegar | ½ small bunch chives | ½ cup cottage cheese | 1 cup vegetable broth | 1 ⅓ cups spelt | ½ leek | 2 small carrots | 4 TBSP sunflower oil | 2 eggs | ¼ TSP curry powder | 4 nice lettuce leaves | 8 radishes | 4 whole wheat buns (page 20) | 1 cucumber | Salt and freshly ground black pepper*

CUCUMBER

8 Wash the lettuce leaves and shake dry.

10 Wash the cucumber, wipe dry, and cut into slices.

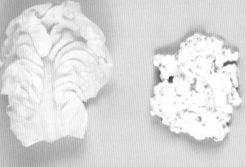

11 Cut the rolls in half, lightly toast the insides.

COTTAGE CHEESE

HEALTH CITY

  4 **S**

2 + 3 Wash chives, shake dry, and cut small. | Mix the cottage cheese with chives and salt and pepper to taste.

1

Wash the sprouts well, pat dry with paper towels, marinate in grape seed oil and herb vinegar, and season with salt and pepper.

⑫ STACKING

⑫ STACKING

Place lettuce on the bottoms of the buns, layer the cottage cheese on it, add cucumbers and radishes. Put down the patties, garnish with sprouts, and complete with the covers.

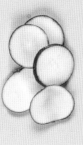

RADISHES

SPROUTS

9

Clean the radishes, wash, pat dry, and cut into thin slices.

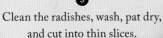

4

Heat the vegetable broth in a pot, add the spelt grain, bring to a boil, remove from heat, and let sit for 10 minutes.

SPELT

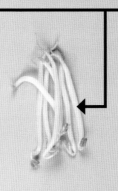

5 — 7

Wash and clean leeks and carrots. Cut the leeks into thin strips, dice the carrots, then sauté in 1 TBSP sunflower oil in a pan. | Mix the vegetables with the grains, two beaten eggs, curry, salt, and pepper, and form four equal-sized patties. | Heat the remaining sunflower oil in a pan and then cook the patties over medium heat for 5 minutes on both sides until crispy. Drain on paper towels.

BOY, COME HOME SOON

2 COOKED RED BEETS

2 TSP RED WINE VINEGAR

4 TSP SUNFLOWER OIL

1 LB. SMOKED PORK

2 MEDIUM-SIZED FIRM COOKING POTATOES

2 EGGS

1 small onion

2 LARGE PICKLES

4 NICE LETTUCE LEAVES

4 BURGER BUNS (PAGE 12)

2 BISMARCK (PICKLED) HERRINGS

½ CUP MAYONNAISE (PAGE 28)

SALT AND FRESH GROUND BLACK PEPPER

1 / Cut the beets into thin slices. **2** / Marinate the red beets overnight in red wine vinegar and sunflower oil, with salt and pepper to taste. **3** / Cut the smoked pork into four equal slices. **4** / Cover the bottom of a medium-sized pot with water, add salt, boil the water, and let the pork slices cook at low heat for 15 minutes. **5** / Peel the potatoes, wash, cut into approximately ⅛ in. thick slices and cook in salted water. **6** / Hard boil the eggs in some water. **7** / Peel the onion and cut it into slices. **8** / Strain the pickles and slice. **9** / Halve the herring fillets. **10** / Shock, peel, and slice the eggs. **11** / Wash the lettuce leaves and shake dry. **12** / Cut the rolls, lightly toast the insides, and brush with mayonnaise. **13** / Lay the lettuce leaves on the bottoms, strain the beets and evenly place along with the pickles, then stack the pork cuts. **14** / Top with the potato slices, one herring fillet, garnish with egg slices and onion rings, and finish with the lids.

BISMARCK-BURGER

 (4) ⅋| S

②
Halve the herring fillets.

⑥ — ⑧
Wash the lettuce leaves and shake dry. | Whisk egg yolk, mustard, vinegar, and lemon juice until creamy. Gradually pour the olive oil and whisk to a smooth emulsion. Season with salt and pepper to taste. | Mix the mayonnaise with the mustard.

EGG

BISMARCK (PICKLED) HERRING

1

Hard boil the eggs in a little water.

INGREDIENTS — *2 eggs | 4 large fillets of Bismarck (pickled) herring | 2 large pickles | 1 small onion | 4 nice lettuce leaves | 1 egg yolk | 1 TSP mustard | 1 splash vinegar | 1 splash lemon juice | 1 cup sunflower oil | Salt and freshly ground black pepper | 2 TBSP spicy mustard | 8 rectangular, large slices pumpernickel*

PICKLE

ONION

5

Shock the eggs, peel, and cut into slices.

3 + **4**

Slice the pickles. | Peel the onion and cut into rings.

9 STACKING

Spread the mayonnaise evenly on the slices of pumpernickel bread. Lay the lettuce leaves on top. Layer the herring, pickles, onions, and egg slices to cover, and complete with the remaining slices of pumpernickel.

DANNEBROG

1 MEDIUM-SIZED ONION
½ BUNCH CHIVES
8 RADISHES
4 green leaf lettuce leaves
2 EGGS
8 SLICES RYE BREAD
¼ CUP SALTED BUTTER
8 FILLETS OF KIPPERS
½ CUP TARTAR SAUCE (PAGE 32)
SALT AND FRESHLY GROUND BLACK PEPPER
CLARIFIED BUTTER FOR FRYING

1 / Peel the onion and cut into rings. **2** / Wash chives, shake dry, and cut fine. **3** / Wash the radish, pat dry, and slice. **4** / Wash the lettuce leaves and shake dry. **5** / Whisk the eggs with salt and pepper seasoning. **6** / Melt 1 TBSP clarified butter in a pan and then let the eggs simmer to scrambled eggs. **7** / Coat the whole grain rye bread with the butter. **8** / Lay the lettuce leaves on the four slices, spread tartar sauce, and lay down two herring fillets. **9** / Then spread the scrambled eggs evenly, garnish with onion rings, radish, and chive, and complete with the other slice of bread. ☛

THE MOUNTAIN CALLS

HASH BROWNS / GROUND BEEF / DRIED BEEF / GRUYÈRE / BACON

INGREDIENTS — *8 large firm russet potatoes | 1 ⅓ LBS. ground beef | 1 pinch of fresh grated nutmeg | 8 slices of bacon | 4 slices Gruyère cheese | 1 garlic clove | ½ bunch chives | 2 parsley branches | 2 branches of thyme | 1 cup watercress | 4 nice iceberg lettuce leaves | ½ cup mayonnaise (page 28) | 8 slices bresaola or prosciutto | Salt and freshly ground black pepper | Clarified butter for frying*

1 / Cook the potatoes for 20 minutes in salted water the day before. The cores should still be uncooked.

2 / Mix the ground meat with ½ TSP salt and ¼ TSP pepper, shape into four equal patties, press a hollow dent into the centers, and refrigerate for 1 hour.

3 / Peel the pre-cooked potatoes, grate on a coarse kitchen grater, season with 1 TSP salt, nutmeg, and pepper.

4 / Heat clarified butter in a large skillet, spread half of the grated potatoes and flatten down with a fork, and cook over medium heat for 5 minutes on both sides until golden.

5 / Cut out four rings (5 in.) and let strain on kitchen paper.

6 / Repeat with the second half of the grated potatoes.

7 / Preheat the oven to 350°F.

8 / Fry the bacon in the pan until crispy.

9 / Sear the patty in clarified butter on both sides and finish cooking in the hot oven for approximately 8 minutes.

10 / About 2 minutes before end of cooking lay the Gruyère cheese slices onto the patties and warm up the potato discs in the oven.

11 / Peel the garlic and finely chop.

12 / Wash and cut the chives into fine rings.

13 / Wash the parsley and thyme, shake dry, pick from the stems and chop finely.

14 / Wash the lettuce leaves and shake dry.

15 / Mix the mayonnaise with garlic, herbs, and the cress, and spread onto the roasted potato discs.

16 / Start by laying the lettuce leaves onto four roasted potato slices, add the cured beef, the patties, bacon, and top with the remaining potato slices.

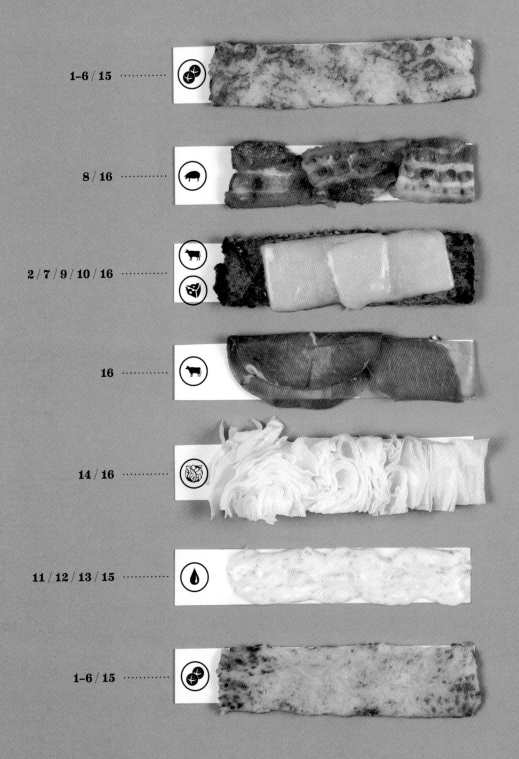

1–6 / 15

8 / 16

2 / 7 / 9 / 10 / 16

16

14 / 16

11 / 12 / 13 / 15

1–6 / 15

INGREDIENTS — *1 lb. veal, prepared kitchen-ready | 2 TBSP flour | 1 egg | 1 cup breadcrumbs | 4 pieces of green asparagus | ½ cup mayonnaise (page 28) | 2 TSP of Worcestershire sauce | 1 TSP mustard | juice of ½ lemon | 4 thin slices cooked ham | 4 thick slices of Emmentaler or Jarlsberg cheese | 4 nice Romaine lettuce leaves | 4 burger buns (page 12) | Salt and freshly ground black pepper | Clarified butter for frying*

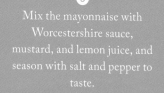

④ Preheat the oven to 350°F.

⑤ Mix the mayonnaise with Worcestershire sauce, mustard, and lemon juice, and season with salt and pepper to taste.

⑨ Wash the lettuce leaves and shake dry.

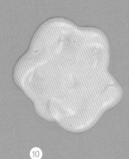

⑩ Halve the rolls and lightly toast the insides. Brush with mayonnaise.

CORDON BLEU BURGER

④ 🍴 M

VEAL TENDERLOIN →

⑪ STACKING

Layer the bottoms of the buns each with a lettuce leaf, set the cordon bleus, garnish with asparagus, and finish with the lids.

③ Blanche the asparagus for about 3 minutes in boiling salt water, then shock in ice water and first cut lengthwise, then across.

① + ② Slice the veal tenderloins into eight equal pieces and flatten lightly. | Season the meat with salt and pepper, dredge in the flour and whisked egg, and then firmly press into the breadcrumbs.

ASPARAGUS

⑥ — ⑧ Sear the veal cuts in clarified butter to golden-brown on both sides. | Place a slice of ham and a slice of Emmentaler or Jarlsberg cheese on four of the tenderloins and cover with the remaining tenderloins. | Heat the cordon bleus in the hot oven for 4 minutes so that the cheese melts somewhat.

HAM

EMMENTALER OR JARLSBERG CHEESE

BROTHER JAKOB

SCALLOPS / SPINACH / PEAS / CARROTS

(4) ⅋|

M

BURGER BUNS   Prepare the burger buns recipe on page 18.

....

CARROT STICKS   Clean the carrots, wash and cut into thin strips. Blanch briefly in salted water, shock right away in cold water, dry thoroughly with a paper towel, and fry in the 325°F hot oil, not too dark.

....

SCALLOPS   Fry the scallops just before stacking in clarified butter over medium heat for 3 minutes on both sides.

....

PEA PUREE   Cook the peas briefly in boiling, salted water, then shock. Process in a blender with crème fraîche to a fine puree and season to taste with salt and pepper.

....

SPINACH   Clean the spinach leaves, wash, shake dry, and marinate with white wine vinegar and grapeseed oil, then season with salt and pepper.

....

MAYONNAISE   Prepare the mayonnaise recipe on page 28. Stir the saffron powder into the white wine, let come to a boil, cool down and mix into the mayonnaise.

....

BURGER BUNS

INGREDIENTS

4 sesame seed buns (page 18)
2 carrots
Oil for deep frying
12 nice scallops
Clarified butter for frying
²/₃ cup peas
2 TBSP crème fraîche
¹/₃ cup spinach
1 TBSP white wine vinegar
3 TBSP grape seed oil
1 pinch saffron powder
¹/₃ cup mayonnaise (page 28)
1 TBSP white wine
Salt and freshly ground black pepper

STACKING   Halve the rolls, lightly toast the insides, and coat the bottoms with saffron mayonnaise. Spread the spinach, then the pea puree, pile on the scallops, and distribute the carrot fritters. Close with the top lids.

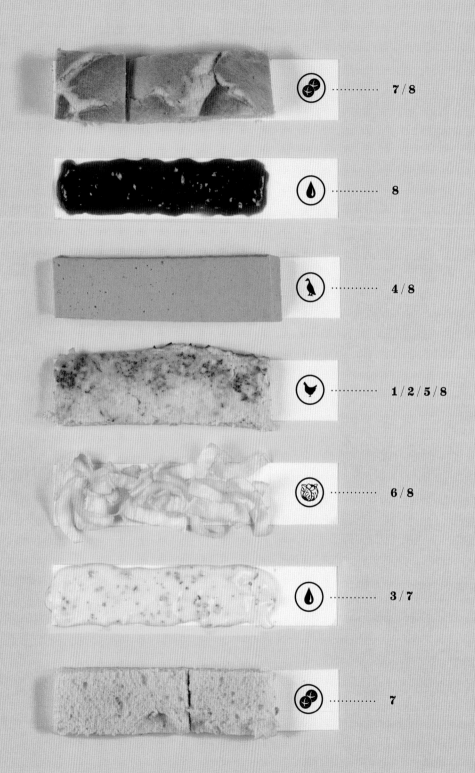

7 / 8

8

4 / 8

1 / 2 / 5 / 8

6 / 8

3 / 7

7

PARIS PARIS

GROUND CHICKEN / TRUFFLE / FOIE GRAS / PLUM

INGREDIENTS — *1 lb. ground chicken | 1 small jar marinated truffle (¼ cup) | 2 TBSP Madeira wine | 2 TBSP red port wine | 1 TBSP cognac | ¼ cup mayonnaise (page 28) | ½ lb. duck foie gras from the jar (delicatessens) | 8 nice yellow chicory leaves | 4 brioche buns (page 11) | 4 TBSP plum chutney (page 30) | Pickle spices | Salt and freshly ground black pepper | Clarified butter for frying*

1 / Mix the ground chicken with ½ TSP salt and ¼ TSP pepper, form four equal patties (about 1/3 in. thick), press hollow indents into the centers, and let cool for 1 hour.

2 / Preheat the oven to 350°F.

3 / Chop the truffle small and bring to a boil with madeira wine, port, cognac, and pickle spices, then cool and mix into the mayonnaise.

4 / Divide the duck foie gras into four equal portions.

5 / Flash fry the patties in clarified butter on both sides and finish by baking in the hot oven for 8 minutes.

6 / Wash the chicory leaves and shake dry.

7 / Halve the buns, lightly toast the insides, and brush the bottoms with truffle mayonnaise.

8 / Place the chicory leaves and the patties, distribute the foie gras, garnish with the plum chutney, and top with the bun's lids.

2 — 4

Whisk the eggs with salt and pepper.| Turn the Camembert in flour, then in egg, and finally carefully in bread crumbs. | Warm plenty of clarified butter in a frying pan and gently heat the Camembert until it is golden brown.

5 + 6

Wash the lettuce leaves and shake dry. | Halve the buns and lightly toast the insides, then coat the undersides with the parsley mayonnaise.

CAMEMBERT

1

Pick the parsley, blanche in salted boiling water, shock in ice water. Pat dry and blend into mayonnaise.

CAMEM-BURGER

INGREDIENTS — *1 bunch parsley | ½ cup mayonnaise (page 28) | 2 eggs | 4 Camembert cheeses, ¼ lb. each | ½ cup flour | 1 cup breadcrumbs | 4 nice red leaf lettuce leaves | 4 whole wheat buns (page 20) | 4 TBSP lingonberry or blackberry jam | 1 cup watercress | clarified butter for frying*

 (4) ¶| S

CRESS

CRANBERRIES

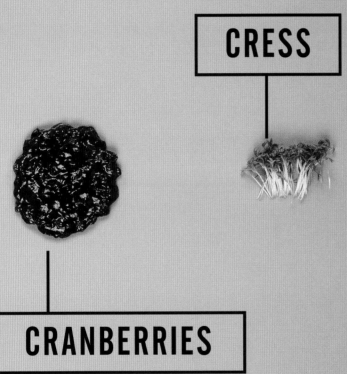

❼ STACKING

Place a leaf of lettuce on the bottom of the buns, layer on the Camembert pieces, spread lingonberry jam, garnish with cress, and complete with the lids.

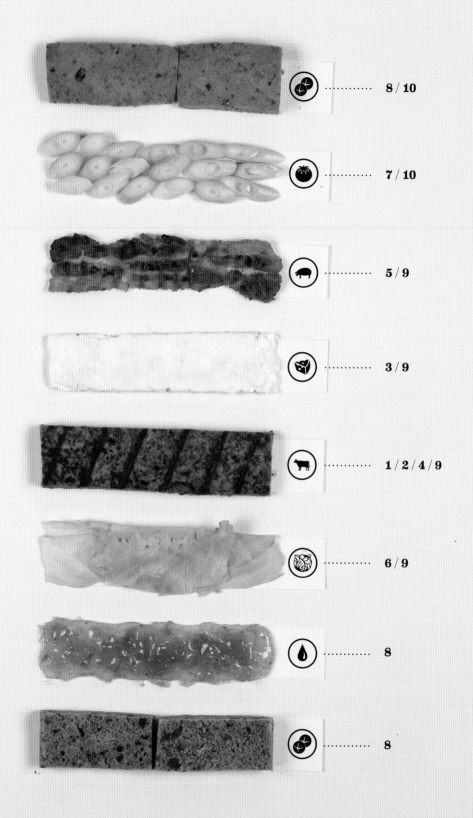

8 / 10

7 / 10

5 / 9

3 / 9

1 / 2 / 4 / 9

6 / 9

8

8

GO BLUES

GROUND BEEF / BLUE CHEESE / BACON / FIG MUSTARD

S

INGREDIENTS — *1 ⅓ lbs. ground beef | ½ lb. Fourme d'Ambert (French blue cheese) | 2 TBSP crème fraîche | 12 slices bacon | 4 nice Iceberg lettuce leaves | 2 scallions | 4 walnut buns (page 21) | 4 TBSP fig mustard (whole grain mustard mixed with fig preserves can be used) | Salt and freshly ground black pepper*

1 / Mix the ground meat, ½ TSP salt, and ¼ TSP pepper, and shape into four equal patties, press a hollow indent into the centers, and let cool in the refrigerator for 1 hour.

2 / Preheat the oven to 350°F.

3 / Blend the cheese and the crème fraîche with a fork, and make four equal parts on parchment paper.

4 / Grill the patties in a pan at high heat on both sides quickly and finish in the hot oven for about 8 minutes.

5 / Fry the bacon in a pan until crispy.

6 / Wash the lettuce leaves and shake dry.

7 / Wash the scallions and cut into fine rings.

8 / Halve the buns and lightly toast the insides. Spread fig mustard on all sides.

9 / Place a leaf of lettuce on the bottom halves, then put down the patties, cover with the cheese and bacon.

10 / Sprinkle scallions and finish with the tops.

TARTARE HALF BAKED

BEEF TENDERLOIN / WILD HERB SALAD / CUCUMBER / CAPERS / ONION

4 🍴

M

BURGER BUNS Prepare the burger bun recipe on page 18.

ONION Peel the onion and cut into rings.

CUCUMBER Wash and slice the cucumber.

TARTARE Chop the beef fillets with a sharp knife. Peel the shallots and cut into fine cubes. Mix the meat with the shallots, olive oil, Worcestershire sauce, parsley, egg yolk, ketchup, and Tabasco and season with ½ TSP salt, ¼ TSP pepper, and the cayenne pepper to a piquant taste. Form four equal tartare patties, press a hollow dent into the centers, and refrigerate for 1 hour. Just before the stacking the burger, fry the patties in some clarified butter for 3 minutes on both sides.

SALAD Wash the leaves and shake dry. Mix a marinade out of oil, vinegar, honey, salt, and pepper, and cover the leaves.

MAYONNAISE Drain the capers well and mix into the mayonnaise.

BURGER BUNS

STACKING Halve the rolls, lightly toast the insides, spread a coat of caper mayonnaise on undersides. Lay the salad, then the patties, and garnish with cucumber and onion rings. Coat the bun's lid with mustard and top the burger.

INGREDIENTS

TARTARE

1 ⅓ lbs. beef tenderloin or hip

2 shallots

2 TBSP Worcestershire sauce

3 TBSP olive oil

3 TBSP ketchup

1 TBSP chopped parsley

1 egg yolk

1 dash Tabasco

1 pinch cayenne pepper

Salt and freshly ground black pepper

Clarified butter for frying

BURGER

3 TBSP capers

¼ cup mayonnaise (page 28)

1 red onion

1 cup wild herb salad

3 TBSP grape seed oil

1 TBSP chardonnay vinegar

1 TSP honey

4 sesame seed buns (page 18)

½ cucumber

4 TBSP dijon mustard

Salt and freshly ground black pepper

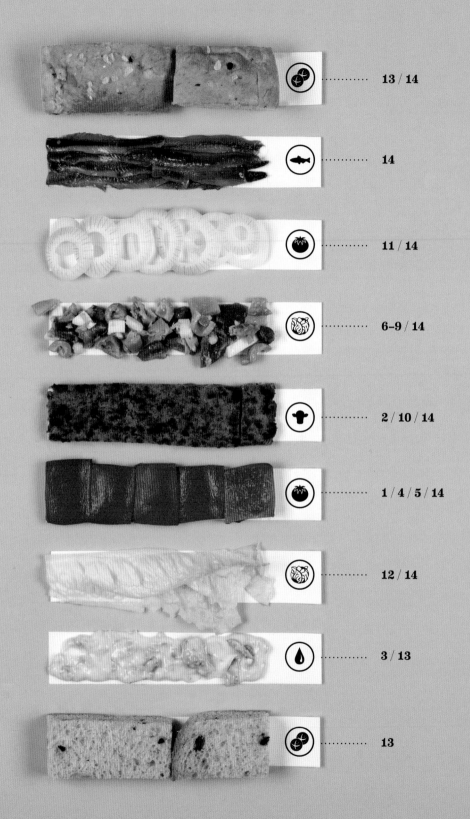

13 / 14

14

11 / 14

6–9 / 14

2 / 10 / 14

1 / 4 / 5 / 14

12 / 14

3 / 13

13

À LA NIÇOISE

GROUND VEAL / TUNA / EGG / ONION / ANCHOVIES

4 ¶|

M

INGREDIENTS — *1 lb. ground veal | 1 can tuna (1 cup) | ½ cup mayonnaise (page 28) | 2 hard boiled eggs | 1 red bell pepper | 10 string beans | 8 cherry tomatoes | 1 TBSP green olives, pitted | 1 TBSP capers | 1 red onion | 4 nice Romaine lettuce leaves | 4 olive focaccia (page 16) | 4 anchovy fillets | Salt and freshly ground black pepper | Olive oil | Clarified butter for frying*

1 / Preheat the oven to 400°F.

2 / Mix the ground meat with ½ TSP salt and ¼ TSP pepper and form four equally large patties. Press a hollow into the centers and refrigerate for 1 hour.

3 / Mix half of the tuna with mayonnaise into a smooth cream.

4 / Wash the peppers, rub dry and bake in hot oven for 10 minutes. Then, remove the skin and seeds and portion into four equal pieces.

5 / Reduce the oven temperature to 350°F.

6 / Blanch the beans in salt water until soft and cut into small pieces.

7 / Wash the cherry tomatoes, wipe dry, and quarter.

8 / Chop the olives and fluff up the remaining tuna.

9 / Mix tuna, beans, tomatoes, olives, capers, and olive oil into a marinade and season with salt and pepper.

10 / Sear the patties in clarified butter on both sides and finish cooking in the oven for approximately 8 minutes.

11 / Peel the onion and cut in rings.

12 / Wash the lettuce leaves and shake dry.

13 / Halve the buns and lightly toast the insides. Coat with the mayonnaise.

14 / Place a lettuce leaf on each of the bottoms, lay the peppers on them and then place the patties. Cover with a good portion of Niçoise salad. Peel the eggs and cut into slices. Garnish with onion rings and anchovy fillets and complete with the buns' lids.

BE HUNGRY—
BE RICH

2 LOBSTERS (ABOUT 1 ⅓ LBS.)

1 ANDALUSIAN TOMATO
(ALTERNATIVELY, VINE-RIPE TOMATO)

1 AVOCADO

1 CUP SEAWEED SALAD

JUICE OF 1 LIME

1 PINCH CAYENNE PEPPER

8 SLICES OF SERRANO HAM

4 NICE ICEBERG LETTUCE LEAVES

4 SQUID INK BUNS (PAGE 17)

½ CUP COCKTAIL SAUCE (PAGE 25)

SALT AND FRESHLY GROUND BLACK PEPPER

OLIVE OIL FOR THE MARINADE AND ROASTING

CLARIFIED BUTTER FOR FRYING

1 / Boil the lobsters in salted water for 4 minutes and remove. **2** / Remove the claws and cook 2 more minutes. Shock in ice water. **3** / Break up the lobsters, open the tails, and remove the intestines, clean the claws, cut in half, and add a small and a half big claw per serving. **4** / Wash and dry the tomato and cut into slices. **5** / Halve the avocado, core and peel, then slice the halves and marinate with salt, pepper, and olive oil. **6** / Flavor the seaweed salad with lime juice, salt, and cayenne pepper. **7** / Gently fry the Serrano ham in olive oil in the pan until crispy. **8** / Heat up the portioned lobster with some clarified butter in a frying pan. **9** / Wash the lettuce leaves and shake dry. **10** / Halve the rolls and lightly toast the insides, then sprinkle with cocktail sauce. **11** / Place the leaves onto the bottoms, add the tomatoes, add the portioned lobster, and spread the seaweed salad evenly on top. **12** / Put the avocado slices, then the Serrano ham on top, and finish with the lids. 👉

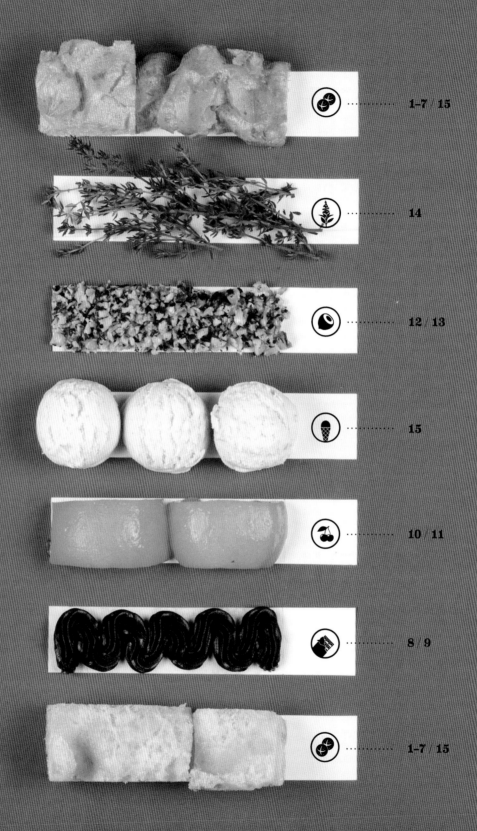

1–7 / 15

14

12 / 13

15

10 / 11

8 / 9

1–7 / 15

PEACH, WIND & CHOCOLATE

CREAM PUFFS / PEACH / CHOCOLATE / VANILLA ICE CREAM

L

INGREDIENTS — CHOUX PASTRY *¼ cup butter | 1 pinch of salt | 1 ¼ cups flour | 4 eggs | 1 pinch baking powder* FILLING *½ cup dark chocolate (55% cocoa content) | ⅔ cup heavy cream | 1 ½ TBSP white sugar | 2 TBSP butter | 2 peaches | 1 cup peach juice | 2 TBSP peach liqueur | Core of ½ vanilla pod | ⅓ cup chopped hazelnuts | 1 ½ TBSP of brown sugar | 2 stems of lemon thyme | 4 scoops vanilla ice cream*

1 / Bring 1 cup of water, butter, and salt to a boil in a saucepan.

2 / Take the pot from the stove, add the flour with a wooden spoon, and stir until smooth.

3 / Put the pot back on the still-hot plate and stir until it comes as a doughy mix off the bottom.

4 / Place the dough in a bowl, let cool off, and, one by one, blend in the eggs.

5 / Now stir in the baking soda and let the dough cool for 5 hours.

6 / Preheat the oven to 400°F and line a baking tray with parchment paper.

7 / Using a pastry bag, squeeze four medium-sized puffs onto the tray and bake in the hot oven for about 20 minutes.

8 / In the meantime, chop up the chocolate.

9 / Boil the cream with half of the sugar, pour over the chopped chocolate, and blend with a hand blender. Process it into a homogeneous mass without incorporating too much air into the mixture, and gradually add 1 TBSP of butter.

10 / Wash, peel, and halve the peaches, and remove the stone.

11 / Caramelize the remaining sugar in a saucepan and deglaze with peach juice and peach liqueur. Add the vanilla seeds and pour the sauce, still cooking, over the peach halves. Allow these to cool.

12 / Lightly toast the hazelnuts in a frying pan while stirring.

13 / Add the brown sugar, then slowly melt the remaining butter in it. Put the brittle onto a baking sheet to cool and break it into big chunks.

14 / Wash the thyme, shake dry, pluck, and chop coarsely.

15 / Cut the cream puffs in half and spread the truffle mass with a pastry bag with a star nozzle. Place the peaches, insides facing up. Put 1 ball of vanilla ice cream into each peach. Sprinkle candied roasted nuts, garnish with thyme, and finish with the lid.

SUNNY SIDE UP

🐄 ④ 🍴 M

1¾ LBS. GROUND BEEF
1 BOK CHOY
1 SMALL ONION
4 TSP SOY SAUCE
1 SMALL JAR MARINATED TRUFFLE OIL (APPROX. 1 OZ.)
4 TSP MADEIRA
4 TSP RED PORT WINE
2 TSP COGNAC
1 TSP TRUFFLE OIL SET ASIDE
¼ CUP CRÈME FRAÎCHE
1 RED ONION
4 nice red leaf lettuce leaves
4 EGGS (SIZE L)
4 SESAME SEED BUNS (PAGE 18)
4 TBSP BARBECUE SAUCE (PAGE 23)
SALT AND FRESH GROUND
BLACK PEPPER
CLARIFIED BUTTER FOR FRYING

1 / Mix the ground meat with ½ TSP salt and ¼ TSP pepper, form four equally sized patties *(approx. ⅔ in. thick)*, and press a hollow indent into the centers. Refrigerate for 1 hour. **2** / The bok choy is washed and roughly cut into strips. **3** / Peel the onion, cut into small cubes and sauté in some clarified butter, then add the bok choy. Simmer and deglaze with the soy sauce. **4** / Preheat the oven to 250°F. **5** / Chop the truffles and cook up with the madeira wine, port wine, cognac, and truffle oil. **6** / Let the truffles cool and mix in the crème fraîche with salt and pepper to taste. **7** / The red onion is peeled and cut into rings. **8** / Sear the patties on both sides in hot clarified butter and finish in the hot oven for about 8 minutes. **9** / Wash the lettuce leaves and shake dry. **10** / Fry the eggs in some clarified butter in a pan so that the yolks are still liquid; flavor the egg whites with salt and pepper. **11** / Cut the buns in half, lightly toast the insides and coat the bottom with the barbecue sauce. **12** / Lay down the lettuce leaves, distribute the bok choy on them, and place the patties on top. **13** / Layer onion rings, spread the truffle paste, put the eggs on top, and just lean the lid on the burger. 👉

CAPRESE– GEDDIT?

GROUND BEEF / MOZZARELLA / TOMATO / ARUGULA

S

INGREDIENTS — *1 ⅓ lbs. ground beef | 2 balls buffalo mozzarella | 1 ½ cup arugula | 4 TSP aged balsamic vinegar | 2 vine-ripe tomatoes | 4 olive focaccia rolls (page 16) | ½ cup mayonnaise (Page 28) | 4 TBSP pesto (page 29) | Salt and freshly ground black pepper | Olive oil for roasting and marinating*

1 / Mix the ground meat with ½ TSP salt and ¼ TSP pepper. Form four equally large patties (approx. ½ in. thick) and indent the middles with a spoon. Let cool for about 1 hour.

2 / Preheat the oven to 350°F.

3 / Sear the patties in olive oil from both sides, then finish in the hot oven, cooking for approximately 8 minutes.

4 / Cut the mozzarella into slices. Marinate with salt, pepper, and olive oil.

5 / Rinse the arugula. Season with olive oil, 2 TSP balsamic vinegar, salt, and pepper.

6 / Tomatoes are rinsed, cored, and sliced.

7 / Cut the buns in half and lightly toast the insides.

8 / Mix the mayonnaise with the remaining balsamic and spread on the bottoms.

9 / Distribute the arugula, lay down the tomato slices, set the patties on them, and round it out with the mozzarella slices and 1 TBSP of the pesto garnish. Finish with the burger tops.

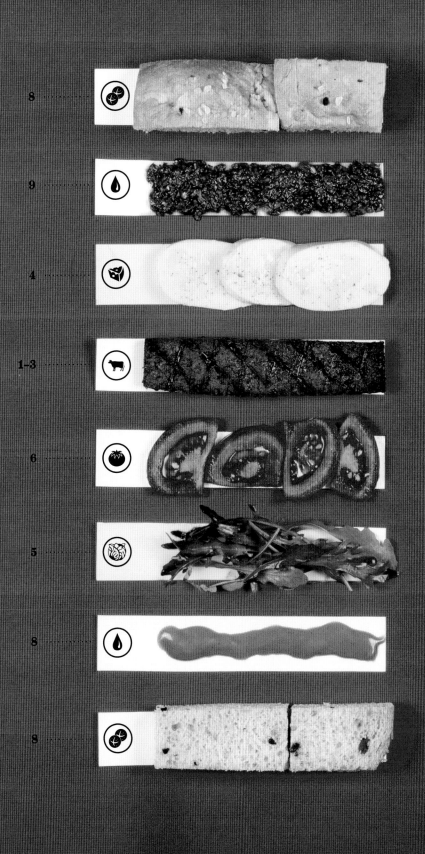

THE ITALIAN JOB

SMOKED BEEF BRISKET / HAM / BURRATA / ARUGULA / TOMATO

S

INGREDIENTS — *4 vine-ripe tomatoes | 1 garlic clove | 2 stems of thyme | 2 TBSP olive oil | ½ cup arugula | 2 TSP balsamic vinegar | 4 tomato buns (page 19) | 8 TBSP salsa verde (Page 31) | 16 slices pastrami (smoked beef brisket) | 2 medium Burrata (Italian cheese similar to mozzarella) | 4 slices of Culatello or prosciutto | Salt and freshly ground black pepper*

1 / Preheat the oven to 175°F.

2 / Wash the tomatoes, dry, and slice.

3 / Peel the garlic and cut it into thin slices.

4 / Wash the thyme, shake the leaves dry, and pluck them off.

5 / Line a baking tray with parchment paper and the tomato slices on it, drizzle some olive oil, salt, and pepper, and sprinkle thyme and garlic and let dry in the oven for about 1 hour.

6 / Rinse the arugula, shake dry and marinate with balsamic vinegar and olive oil, and season with salt and pepper to taste.

7 / Cut the buns in half, lightly toast the insides, and coat with 1 TBSP salsa verde.

8 / Distribute the tomatoes on the bottom halves and give each burger four slices of the pastrami.

9 / Halve the Burrata and lay, with the cut side up, on the pastrami. Add salt and pepper to taste.

10 / Spread the arugula evenly on the Burrata, give each a slice of Culatello, and finish by placing the bun on top.

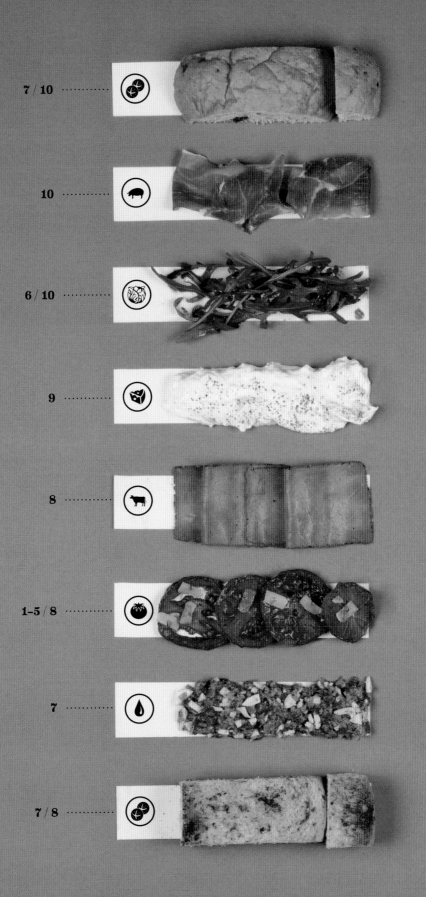

7 / 10 ·········

10 ·········

6 / 10 ·········

9 ·········

8 ·········

1–5 / 8 ·········

7 ·········

7 / 8 ·········

①
Preheat the oven to 175°F.

② — ⑤
Wash the tomatoes, rub dry, and slice. | Wash the herbs, shake dry, and pluck the leaves from the branches. | Peel the garlic and finely slice. | Line a baking tray with parchment paper, distribute the tomato slices on it, drizzle with olive oil, season with salt and pepper, and sprinkle with thyme, rosemary, and garlic. Dust with a little powdered sugar and let dry in the oven for 1 hour.

⑦ — ⑨
As soon as the tomatoes come out of the oven, increase the baking temperature to 350°F. | Cut the jalapeños in fine rings. | Wash the arugula, shake dry, sprinkle with olive oil and a little balsamic vinegar as marinade, with salt and pepper.

ARUGULA

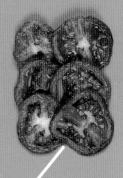

⑫
Cut the rolls in half and lightly toast the insides. Sprinkle with aioli.

TOMATOES

INGREDIENTS — *4 vine-ripe tomatoes | 1 thyme sprig | 1 sprig of rosemary | 1 garlic clove | 2 TBSP olive oil | 1 TSP powdered sugar | 1 ½ lbs. ground beef | ¼ TSP cayenne pepper | 4 pickled jalapeños | ½ cup arugula | 3 TBSP olive oil | 1 TBSP balsamic | 4 slices cheddar | 4 tomato buns (page 19) | ⅓ cup aioli (page 22) | 16 slices crisp chorizo | Salt and freshly ground black pepper | Clarified butter for frying | Powdered sugar for dusting*

(6) Mix the ground beef with ½ TSP salt and the cayenne pepper. Form four equally large patties (approx. ⅔ in. thick). Press a hole in the centers and refrigerate for 1 hour.

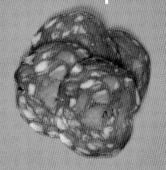

(13) STACKING

Rinse the arugula and spread on the bottoms of the buns. Lay down tomato slices, then the oven-baked patties. Garnish with chorizo and conclude with the lids.

(10) + (11) Sear the patties in clarified butter on both sides and finish in the hot oven for about 8 minutes. | About 2 minutes before the end of cooking put the jalapeños on the patties, then a slice of cheddar on top.

CHORIZO

GROUND BEEF

MUY
CALIENTE

  (4) M

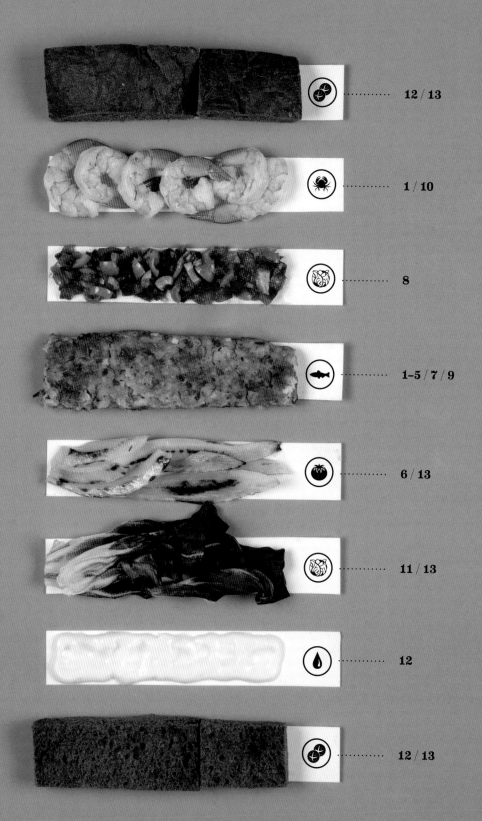

12 / 13

1 / 10

8

1–5 / 7 / 9

6 / 13

11 / 13

12

12 / 13

PRAWNY

SHRIMP / FENNEL / RADICCHIO / OLIVE

INGREDIENTS — *1 ⅓ lbs. medium-sized shrimp, kitchen-ready | 1 large red chili pepper | 2 scallions | 1 garlic clove | ¼ TSP cayenne pepper | 1 TBSP chervil, destemmed | ½ TSP tarragon, destemmed | ½ cup bread crumbs | 1 egg | Juice and zest of ½ lemon | 1 small fennel bulb | 8 cherry tomatoes | 10 green olives without stone | 4 leaves radicchio | 4 squid ink buns (page 17) | ½ cup mayonnaise (page 28, but replace half of the oil with sweet almond oil) | Salt and freshly ground black pepper | Olive oil for the marinade | Clarified butter for frying*

1 / Set four of the shrimp aside, finely chop the rest.

2 / Core the chili and cut into small cubes.

3 / Clean the scallions, wash, and cut into fine rings.

4 / Peel and finely chop the garlic.

5 / Mix the chopped shrimp well with ½ TSP salt, cayenne pepper, chili, scallions, garlic, chervil, tarragon, bread crumbs, egg, and lemon juice, and form four equal-sized patties. Press an indentation into the middles and refrigerate 1 hour.

6 / Clean, wash, and cut fennel into slices, and flash fry in the pan on both sides. Marinate it with salt, olive oil, and pepper.

7 / Preheat the oven to 350°F.

8 / Wash the cherry tomatoes, halve, and core stem. Chop small along with the olives, and season with salt, pepper, and olive oil to taste.

9 / Lightly sauté the patties in clarified butter on both sides and finish in the hot oven, cooking for approximately 10 minutes to finish.

10 / In the meantime, roast the four remaining shrimp in a little clarified butter and season with salt.

11 / Wash the lettuce leaves and shake dry.

12 / Cut the buns in half, lightly toast the insides, and spread with a coat of mayonnaise.

13 / Layer the bottoms with a leaf of lettuce, the fennel, the patties, then spread on the tomato-olive salad. Set down two shrimp halves and finish by leaning the lid on top.

THE OLD GREEK

GROUND LAMB / FETA / YOGURT / WHITE CABBAGE / BELL PEPPER

M

INGREDIENTS — *1 ⅓ lbs. ground lamb meat | ¼ TSP paprika powder | ¼ TSP gyro spice | 1 cup feta cheese | ¼ cup pickles | 4 cloves of garlic | ½ cup of Greek yogurt | 2 TSP olive oil | ¼ small cabbage | 2 TBSP white wine vinegar | 2 TBSP olive oil for the marinade | 1 green bell pepper | 2 vine-ripe tomatoes | 1 small onion | 1 TBSP green olives, pitted | 1 pinch oregano | 2 red peppers | 4 pieces of pita bread | Salt and freshly ground black pepper | Olive oil for roasting and marinating*

1 / Mix the ground lamb meat with ½ TSP salt, ¼ TSP pepper, paprika, and the gyro spices. Form four equally large patties. Press an indent in the middles and set cold for approximately 1 hour.

2 / Portion the feta into four equal slices and marinate with olive oil.

3 / Grate the pickles.

4 / Peel the garlic cloves and finely chop, but set side 1 clove of garlic.

5 / Make the tzatziki of yogurt, cucumber, three of the chopped garlic cloves, and add olive oil, salt, and pepper to taste.

6 / Preheat the oven to 400°F.

7 / Cut the cabbage into thin strips, mix well in a marinade of olive oil and white wine vinegar.

8 / Now wash, clean, and dice the green pepper and the tomatoes finely.

9 / Peel the onion and also dice finely.

10 / Chop olives.

11 / Mix peppers, tomatoes, onion, remaining garlic, and olives into the cabbage and season with salt, pepper, and oregano.

12 / Cook the red peppers in the hot oven for 10 minutes, peel off skin, remove seeds, and divide into four equal pieces.

13 / Reduce the temperature of the oven to 350°F.

14 / Sear the patties on both sides in olive oil and finish cooking in the oven for 10 minutes.

15 / About two minutes before end of cooking add the feta slices.

16 / Meanwhile, bake the pita bread in the toaster, cut, and sprinkle with tzatziki.

17 / For each, pile on one heaping tablespoon of the white coleslaw, lay on the patty, garnish with red pepper, and finish with the bread tops.

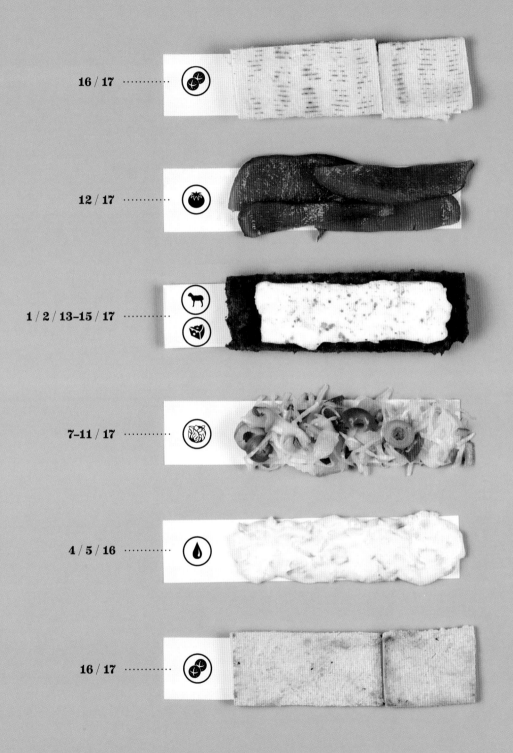

16 / 17

12 / 17

1 / 2 / 13–15 / 17

7–11 / 17

4 / 5 / 16

16 / 17

TSAR NIKOLAJ

🐟 ④ 🍴 M

1 LB. FRESH SALMON FILLET
1 SHALLOT / 1 EGG
2 TBSP BREADCRUMBS
½ CUP CRÈME FRAÎCHE
JUICE OF 1 LIME
¼ LB. BALIK SALMON "TSAR NIKOLAJ"
(ALTERNATIVELY, SMOKED SALMON)
4 LETTUCE LEAVES
8 LARGE BLINTZES (PAGE 10)
4 TSP OSIETRA CAVIAR
4 DILL TIPS
SALT AND CAYENNE PEPPER
CLARIFIED BUTTER FOR FRYING

1 / Cut the fresh salmon in slices and chop finely. **2** / Peel and finely dice the shallots. **3** / Mix the salmon with the shallot, egg, breadcrumbs, ½ TSP salt, and ¼ TSP cayenne pepper, shape into four equal-sized patties, indent them in the middles, and refrigerate 1 hour. **4** / Mix the crème fraîche with the lime juice and salt and cayenne pepper to taste. **5** / Cut the Balik or smoked salmon into thin slices. **6** / Fry the patties in clarified butter over medium heat on both sides for about 4 minutes. **7** / Wash the lettuce leaves and shake dry. **8** / Coat the four blintzes with half of the crème fraîche, then place the salad leaves, the patties, then the Balik salmon. Give each an additional TBSP creme fraîche and garnish with caviar and dill tips. **9** / Finally, place the remaining four blintzes on the burger. 👉

BREAKFAST @TIFFANY'S

BRATWURST / EGGS / BACON / CHEESE / TOMATO

4 🍴

S

BURGER BUNS   Prepare the burger bun recipe on page 20.

....

CHESTER CHEESE

....

TOMATOES   Wash the tomatoes, remove the cores, and cut the tomatoes into slices.

....

BRATWURSTS   Fry the sausages in clarified butter until golden brown, then halve lengthwise.

....

PANCAKES   Whisk the eggs with salt, pepper, and a splash of milk. Heat some clarified butter in a frying pan and leave the eggs to cook over medium heat. Then cut the pancake into quarters.

....

BACON   Fry the bacon in the pan until crispy.

....

SALAD   Wash the lettuce leaves and shake dry.

....

BURGER BUNS

INGREDIENTS

4 whole wheat buns (page 20)

4 slices Chester (gouda or American are alternatives)

2 medium-sized vine-ripe tomatoes

3–4 bratwursts

Clarified butter for frying

4 eggs

1 TSP milk

12 slices bacon

4 green leaf lettuce leaves

2 spreadable cheese wedges

Salt and freshly ground black pepper

STACKING   Cut the buns in half, lightly toast the insides, and evenly distribute the cheese spread. Give each a lettuce leaf and three slices of bacon. Then, one by one, place the pancakes, the halved sausages, the tomato slices, and the chester cheese. Complete them with the lids.

CREAM AND CHEESE

🐄 ④ 🍴 ⌐S⌐

2 LBS. GROUND BEEF
1 LIME
1 GARLIC CLOVE
1 GREEN BELL PEPPER
⅔ CUP CREAM CHEESE
1 TSP OF ROASTED SESAME
1 RED ONION
4 JALAPEÑOS
4 SLICES OF CHEDDAR
4 radicchio leaves
4 TOMATO ROLLS (PAGE 19)
SALT AND FRESHLY GROUND BLACK PEPPER
CLARIFIED BUTTER FOR FRYING

1 / Mix the ground meat with ½ TSP salt and ¼ TSP pepper, form four equal-sized patties, create a hollow in each middle with a spoon, and refrigerate for 1 hour. **2** / Peel the lime, cut into segments, and discard the membrane. **3** / Peel the garlic and finely chop. **4** / Wash the pepper, rub dry, clean, and cut into small cubes. **5** / Mix the fresh cream cheese with lime segments, garlic, peppers, and sesame, and season to taste with salt and pepper. **6** / Preheat the oven to 350°F. **7** / Peel the red onion and cut into slices. **8** / Cut the jalapeños into rings. **9** / Sear the patties on both sides in clarified butter, then finish in the hot oven for about 10 minutes. **10** / About 2 minutes before end of cooking time, add the jalapeños and the slices of cheese. **11** / Wash the lettuce leaves and shake dry. **12** / Halve the rolls, lightly toast the insides, and thinly coat with the cream cheese. **13** / Lay the lettuce leaves onto the bottoms, then the remaining cream cheese, the patties, garnish with onion rings, and top off with the lids. 👉

THE BIG APPLE

DUCK BREAST / CELERY / WALNUT / APPLE / PINEAPPLE

BURGER BUNS   Prepare the burger buns recipe on page 21.

DUCK BREAST   Preheat the oven to 350°F. Free the duck breast of fat and tendons, cut into the meat crosswise with a knife, and season on both sides with salt and pepper. Heat some clarified butter in an oven-safe pan and fry the two duck breasts. Let the fattier side cook off over lower heat for a little longer. Finish cooking the meat in the hot oven for 8 minutes, then let it rest, and cut into slices.

WALDORF SALAD   Peel the celeriac and cut into about 1 in. long strips, cook for at least 3 minutes in boiling salted water, and shock cool right away. Peel the apples, core, and cut into fine strips. Coarsely chop the walnuts and mix with apple and celery. Blend lemon juice, pineapple syrup, and half of the mayonnaise, season with salt and cayenne pepper to taste, and cover the apple-celery-walnut mixture.

PINEAPPLE RINGS

CHICORY   Wash the endive leaves and shake dry.

BURGER BUNS

INGREDIENTS

4 walnut buns (page 21)

4 duck breasts, about 1/3 lb. each

Clarified butter for frying

½ cup celeriac (celery root)

2 apples (such as Granny Smith)

1/3 cup walnuts

Juice from ½ lemon

1 TBSP pineapple syrup

½ cup mayonnaise (page 28, but replace 4 TSP oil with 4 TSP walnut oil)

1 pinch of cayenne pepper

1 can pineapple rings

8 yellow endive leaves

Salt and freshly ground black pepper

STACKING   Cut the buns in half and spread the remaining mayonnaise. Place two leaves of chicory greens and a slice of pineapple on the bottom halves, then 1 heaping TSBP of Waldorf salad into each of the interiors of the rings. Place the duck breasts and finish with the burger tops.

CLUB BURGER

CHICKEN BREAST / BACON / TOMATO / CUCUMBER

INGREDIENTS — *1 ⅓ lbs. chicken breast | 12 slices bacon | 2 medium-sized vine-ripe tomatoes | 4 crisp iceberg lettuce leaves | 4 sesame seed buns (page 18) | ½ cup mayonnaise (page 28) | 16 slices cucumber with peel on | Salt and freshly ground black pepper | Clarified butter for frying*

1 / Preheat the oven to 350°F.

2 / Season the chicken breast with salt and pepper in 1 TBSP clarified butter and sauté over medium heat until golden brown and finish by baking in the hot oven, 5 minutes on both sides.

3 / Fry the bacon to crispy in a skillet.

4 / Wash the tomatoes and rub dry, sliced, but not too thinly.

5 / Wash the lettuce leaves and shake dry.

6 / Halve the buns, lightly toast, and coat the insides with mayonnaise.

7 / Put a lettuce leaf on the bottom, then cover with cucumber slices.

8 / Cut the warm chicken breasts diagonally into uniform slices and spread on the bread.

9 / Place three slices of bacon and three slices of tomato, and complete with the burger tops.

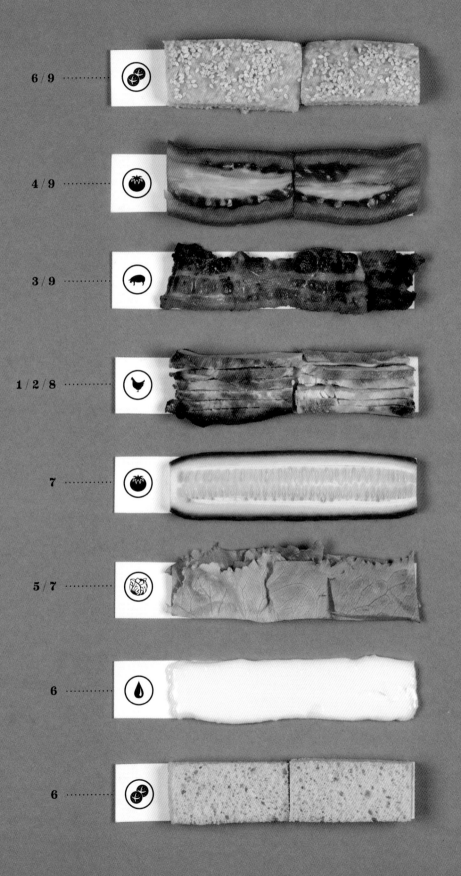

CAESAR BURGER

🐔 ④ 🍴 S̲

1 onion
1 1/3 LBS. GROUND TURKEY BREAST
2 TSP WORCESTERSHIRE SAUCE
2 EGGS
8 ROMAINE SALAD LEAVES
4 OLIVE FOCACCIA (PAGE 16)
CAESAR DRESSING (PAGE 24, TO MAKE THE DRESSING AS THICK AS POSSIBLE, INCREASE OIL BY 1/4 CUP)
8 ANCHOVY FILLETS
1/4 CUP PARMESAN
1/2 AVOCADO
salt and freshly ground black pepper
CLARIFIED BUTTER FOR FRYING

1 / Peel and finely dice the onion. **2** / Mix the ground meat with onions, Worcestershire sauce, 1/2 TSP salt, and 1/4 TSP pepper, form four equal-sized patties *(approx. 1/2 in. thick)*, press a hollow indent into the middle, and refrigerate for 1 hour. **3** / Hard-boil the eggs. **4** / Preheat the oven to 350°F. **5** / Shock cool the eggs, peel, and slice. **6** / Fry the patties with 1 TBSP clarified butter in a pan and finish in hot oven for 8 minutes. **7** / Peel and slice avocado. **8** / Wash the lettuce leaves and shake dry. **9** / Cut the buns in half, lightly toast the insides, and coat with 1 TBSP Caesar dressing. **10** / Place the salad leaves on the bottoms, again some dressing, spread egg and avocado, place the patties, then top with two anchovy fillets. **11** / Finish with grated parmesan and top with the lids. 👉

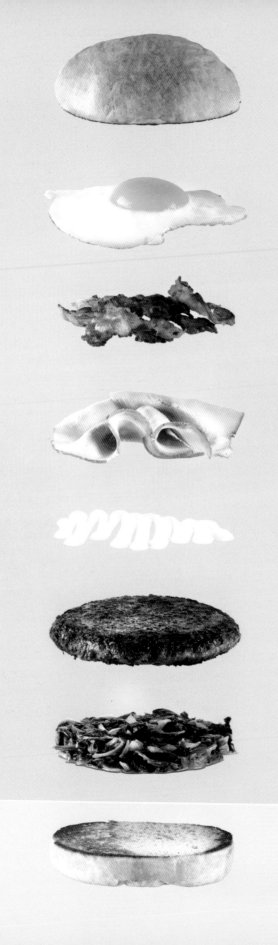

BENEDĪCT BURGER

VEAL / HAM / EGG / BACON / SPĪNACH

4 ⓘ M

BURGER BUNS Prepare the burger bun recipe from page 12.

FRIED EGGS Fry the eggs into clarified butter.

BACON Fry the bacon until crispy.

COOKED HAM

HOLLANDAISE SAUCE Prepare the hollandaise sauce recipe from page 27.

PATTY Mix the ground veal with ½ TSP salt and ¼ TSP pepper and form four equally large patties (approx. ½ in. thick). Press a hollow into the middles with a spoon and set to cool for 1 hour. In the meantime, preheat the oven to 350°F. Heat the clarified butter in an oven-safe pan, sear the patties from both sides and finish cooking in the hot oven for approximately 8 minutes.

SPINACH Peel and dice the shallots into small cubes. Fry the diced shallots in 1 TBSP clarified butter, add salt, pepper, and nutmeg to the spinach, cook briefly, and strain.

BURGER BUNS

ĪNGREDĪENTS

4 burger buns (recipe on page 12)

4 small eggs

Clarified butter for frying

12 slices bacon

4 slices cooked ham

½ cup Hollandaise (recipe on page 27)

1 lb. ground veal

1 shallot

²⁄₃ cup spinach

1 pinch of freshly grated nutmeg

Salt and freshly ground black pepper

STACKING Halve the buns, lightly toast the insides, and spread spinach on the bottoms. Place the patties, ham, and bacon, then dribble a big tablespoon of Hollandaise over everything and top with the fried eggs. Place the bun's top on the burgers.

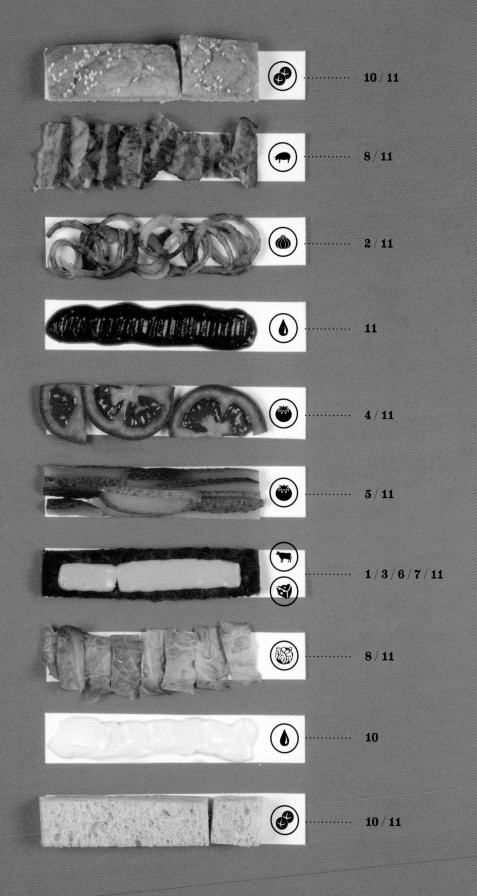

10 / 11

8 / 11

2 / 11

11

4 / 11

5 / 11

1 / 3 / 6 / 7 / 11

8 / 11

10

10 / 11

HEY COWBOY

GROUND BEEF / CHEDDAR / BACON / PICKLES / TOMATOES

4

S

INGREDIENTS — *1 ¾ lbs. ground beef | 2 onions | 2 vine-ripe tomatoes | 2 pickles | 4 slices cheddar | 12 slices bacon | 4 Romaine lettuce leaves | 4 sesame buns (Page 18) | 4 TBSP mayonnaise (page 28) | 4 TBSP barbecue sauce (Page 23) | Salt and freshly ground black pepper | Flour for dusting | Oil for deep-frying | Clarified butter for frying*

1 / Mix the ground meat with ½ TSP salt and ¼ TSP pepper, form four equal burger patties, and push an indent into the centers. Refrigerate for 1 hour.

2 / Peel the onions and cut into rings, sprinkle with flour, and fry until golden in 325°F hot oil. Drip dry on kitchen paper and salt lightly.

3 / Preheat the oven to 350°F.

4 / Wash, dry, core, and slice the tomatoes.

5 / Slice the pickles.

6 / Sear the patties in clarified butter on both sides and finish cooking in the hot oven for about 12 minutes.

7 / Add the cheddar about two minutes before the end of cooking.

8 / In the meantime, pan fry the bacon until crispy.

9 / Wash the lettuce leaves and shake dry.

10 / Cut the buns in half, lightly toast the insides, and spread 1 TBSP mayonnaise on the bases.

11 / Lay down the lettuce leaves, then the patties, pickles, and the tomatoes. Cover with 1 TBSP barbecue sauce and the onion rings. Garnish with the bacon slices and finish with the lids.

FARMER'S LUNCH

I ²/₃ LBS. GROUND BEEF
1 SMALL CAN CORN (APPROX. 10 OZ.)
²/₃ cup of guacamole (page 26)
½ CUP BARBECUE SAUCE (PAGE 23)
I SWEET POTATO
12 SLICES OF BACON
4 ICEBERG LETTUCE LEAVES
4 TOMATO SANDWICHES (PAGE 19)
12 SLICES CUCUMBER
SALT AND FRESHLY GROUND BLACK PEPPER
BUTTER FOR FRYING

1 / Mix the ground meat with ½ TSP salt and ¼ TSP pepper and form four equal patties. Make an indent in the middles with a spoon and refrigerate for 1 hour. **2** / Preheat the oven to 350°F. **3** / Drain the corn and mix into the guacamole. **4** / Sear the patties on both sides in clarified butter, brush each with 1 TBSP barbecue sauce, and cook in the hot oven for 10 minutes. **5** / In the meantime, slice the sweet potatoes *(approx. ⅛ in. thick)* and grill in a pan on both sides. Season with salt and pepper. **6** / Pan fry the bacon until crispy. **7** / Wash the lettuce leaves and shake dry. **8** / Cut the buns in half, lightly toast the insides, and spread guacamole on the bases. **9** / Now place the lettuce leaves, then the sweet potato slices, then the patties, and garnish with cucumber and bacon. **10** / Spread 1 TBSP barbecue sauce onto the burger lids and place on top to finish. 🤏

INGREDIENTS — *1 ⅓ LBS. ground beef | 1 can kidney beans (8 oz.) | 1 medium-sized onion | ½ cup bacon | 1 garlic clove | 1 TSP olive oil | 1 pinch cayenne pepper | 1 papaya | 1 red onion | 2 large red chili peppers | 4 slices cheddar | 4 red leaf lettuce leaves | ½ cup mayonnaise (page 28) | Tabasco to taste | 4 tomato buns (page 19) | Salt and freshly ground black pepper | Clarified butter for frying*

1

Mix the ground beef with ½ TSP salt and ¼ TSP pepper, and shape into four equally large patties. Press an indent into the middles and refrigerate for 1 hour.

GROUND BEEF

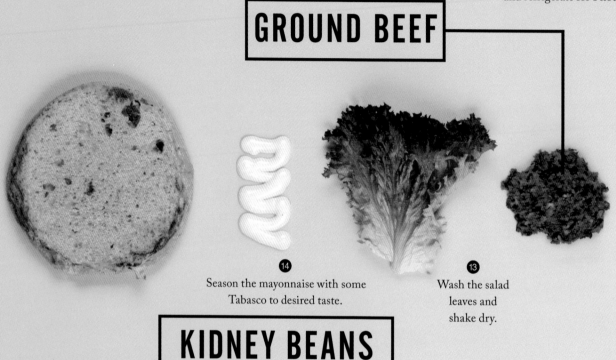

14

Season the mayonnaise with some Tabasco to desired taste.

13

Wash the salad leaves and shake dry.

KIDNEY BEANS

2 — 6

Drain the kidney beans in a strainer. | Peel the onion and dice finely. | Cut the bacon into small cubes. | Peel the garlic and chop finely. | Heat the olive oil in a frying pan, sauté the onions, bacon, and garlic in it, stir in the drained beans, season with salt and cayenne pepper, let cook, and mix with a hand blender.

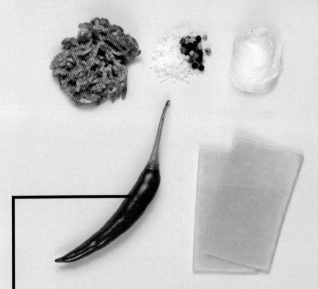

RED HOT CHILI BURGER

🐄 + 🐖 ④ 🍴 M̲

❶❶ + ❶❷

Sear the patties in clarified butter on both sides and bake in the hot oven for 9 minutes. | About 2 minutes before the end of the cooking time add the chili rings and the cheese.

 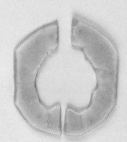  

CHILI

PAPAYA

❶❺

Cut the rolls in half, lightly toast the insides, and spread with the spicy mayonnaise.

❼ — ❶⓪

Preheat the oven to 350°F. | Peel the papaya, cut in half, core, and cut into slices. | Peel the red onion and cut into rings. | Wash the chilies and cut into rings.

❶❻ STACKING

Lay the lettuce leaves on the bottoms of the buns, distribute 1 good TBSP bean paste each, then place the patties, garnish with papaya and onion rings, and finish with the lids.

SMOKER'S EMPIRE

GROUND BEEF / ONION / PEPPER / PICKLES / BACON

INGREDIENTS — *1 ⅔ lbs. ground beef | 4 onions | 4 TSP whisky | 2 pickles | 2 red peppers | 12 slices of smoked bacon | 4 Romaine lettuce leaves | 4 sesame buns (page 18) | ½ cup mayonnaise (page 28, but replace 4 TSP oil with 4 TSP of vegetable oil with a smoky flavor) | 2 TBSP tomato paste | 1 TBSP mustard | Salt and freshly ground black pepper | Clarified butter for frying | Beech chips for smoking*

1 / Mix the ground meat with ½ TSP salt and ¼ TSP pepper and form four big patties. Press a hollow indent into the middles. Cold smoke in a smoker or in a pot with beech chips for 6 minutes, then refrigerate for 1 hour.

2 / Peel the onions and cut into strips.

3 / In a frying pan heat 1 TBSP clarified butter, sauté the onions in it, deglaze with the whisky, and cook down until dark.

4 / Preheat the oven to 350°F.

5 / Drain the pickles and slice.

6 / Wash the peppers, free from stem, and core and cut into strips.

7 / Sear the patties in clarified butter on both sides and finish cooking in the hot oven for about 10 minutes.

8 / Fry the bacon in a pan until crispy.

9 / Wash the lettuce leaves and shake dry.

10 / Cut the buns in half and lightly toast the insides.

11 / Mix the mayonnaise with ketchup and mustard and spread on the bottom halves.

12 / Lay down the salad leaves, 1 TBSP sautéed onion each, spread the peppers, place the patties, and garnish with pickles and bacon. Finish with the lids.

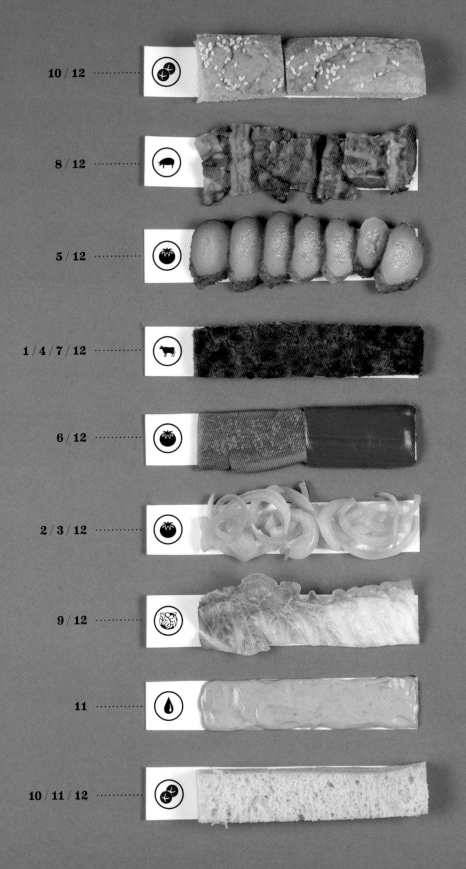

10 / 12 ....

8 / 12 ....

5 / 12 ....

1 / 4 / 7 / 12 ....

6 / 12 ....

2 / 3 / 12 ....

9 / 12 ....

11 ....

10 / 11 / 12 ....

GO YELLOW

🐓 ④ 🍴 M

1 SMALL ONION
1 ⅔ LBS. GROUND CHICKEN GROUND
2 TBSP SWEET SOY SAUCE
1 PINCH CUMIN
1 LARGE ORANGE
2 YELLOW PEPPERS
½ CUP FINE YELLOW FRISÉE SALAD LEAVES
4 CURRY-CHILI BUNS (PAGE 13)
1/2 CUP MAYONNAISE [PAGE 28]
1 TSP INDIAN CURRY POWDER
1 TSP TURMERIC
JUICE OF 1/2 LIME
Olive oil for brushing
CLARIFIED BUTTER FOR FRYING

1 / Peel and finely dice the onion. **2** / Mix the ground meat with ½ TSP salt, ¼ TSP pepper, the onion, soy sauce, and cumin. Form four equal-sized patties *(approx. ½ in. thick)*, push an indent into the centers, and let cool for 1 hour. **3** / Preheat the oven to 400°F. **4** / Peel and fillet the orange. **5** / Wash the peppers, wipe dry, brush with olive oil, and cook in the hot oven for 10 minutes. **6** / Then, peel the peppers, remove the cores, and cut into rough strips. **7** / Reduce the heat in the oven to 350°F. **8** / Sear the patties on both sides in some clarified butter and finish cooking in the hot oven for about 12 minutes. **9** / Wash the lettuce leaves and shake dry. **10** / Mix the mayonnaise with curry, turmeric, and lime juice. **11** / Cut buns in half, lightly toast the insides, and brush with mayonnaise. **12** / Cover the bottoms with Frisée leaves, lay down the patties, evenly distribute the orange fillets and red pepper strips, and top with the lids. 👉

CRAB
ME GOOD

  4 ¶| M

 6 + **7**
Wash the lettuce leaves and
shake dry. | Cut the rolls in half,
lightly toast the insides, and
coat evenly with the cocktail
sauce.

 2
Sear the cabbage in peanut oil and
deglaze with the soy sauce.

1
Wash the bok choy and shake dry.
Cut into rough strips.

BOK CHOY

INGREDIENTS — *1 bok choy | 1 TBSP peanut oil | 4 TSP
soy sauce | 1 fresh mango | 1 avocado | 1 lb. shrimp, cooked and
peeled | 1 TBSP rice vinegar | 1 TBSP Mirin (sweet Japanese
rice wine) | 1 TSP chopped cilantro leaves | Juice of ½ lime |
4 iceberg lettuce leaves | 4 squid ink buns (page 17) | ½ cup
cocktail sauce (page 25) | Salt and cayenne pepper*

❽ STACKING

Place the salad leaves on the bun bottoms and add 1 TBSP bok choy to each. Distribute the shrimp salad evenly with a fork, place mango and avocado on top, and complete with the covers.

❺

Rinse the shrimp and pat dry, then mix with the chopped mango, the chopped avocado, lime juice, Mirin, rice vinegar, and coriander. Season with salt and cayenne pepper to a spicy taste.

CRAB

❸ + ❹

Peel the mango, cut out four nice slices, and set aside. Chop the rest. | Repeat with the avocado.

AVOCADO

MANGO

AVOTUNA BURGER

TUNA FISH / WILD HERB SALAD / AVOCADO

BURGER BUNS Prepare the burger buns recipe on page 17.

WILD HERB SALAD Wash the wild herb salad, shake dry and marinate with vinegar and 3 TBSP olive oil, then season with salt and pepper.

LIME MAYONNAISE Squeeze and mix the juice of the second lime into the mayonnaise.

TUNA Cut the fresh tuna fillets in approximately 1 ½ in. thick slices. Clean the scallions and chilies and cut into fine rings. Wash, shake dry, and finely chop the coriander leaves. Create a marinade out of sea salt, brown sugar, oyster sauce, peanut oil, chilies, chili sauce, cilantro, and scallions. Marinate the tuna in it for approximately 6 hours. Just before stacking, take the tuna out of the marinade and blot dry, then sear in a frying pan with 1 TBSP olive oil on all sides, leaving the core translucent. Prepare portions.

AVOCADO Halve and pit the avocados, and remove the pulp from the peel. Mix with mango puree, the juice of a lime, and 4 TBSP olive oil, and turn into a smooth cream in the blender. Season with salt and cayenne pepper.

BURGER BUNS

STACKING Halve the buns and lightly toast the insides. Spread the avocado cream in the bottoms and the lime mayonnaise in the tops of the toasted buns. Distribute the tuna on the avocado cream and garnish with herb salad. Finish with the lids.

INGREDIENTS

4 squid ink buns (page 17)

½ cup wild herbs

1 TBSP raspberry vinegar

8 TBSP olive oil

2 limes

¼ cup mayonnaise (page 28)

1 lb. tuna fillet

4 scallions

2 large red chili peppers

3 cilantro sprigs

3 ½ TBSP coarse sea salt

2 TBSP brown sugar

2 TBSP oyster sauce

2 TBSP peanut oil

2 TBSP sweet chili sauce

2 avocados

2 TBSP mango puree

1 pinch of cayenne pepper

Salt and freshly ground black pepper

THE FAST (FOOD) SAMURAI

INGREDIENTS — *2 lbs. tofu | 2 TBSP soy sauce | 3 TBSP peanut oil | 1 TBSP Mirin (rice wine) | 1 TBSP sake | 1 TBSP rice vinegar | ¼ cup mayonnaise (page 28) | 2 TSP wasabi paste | 1 TBSP sesame oil | 1 TBSP roasted sesame | 1 TBSP chopped cilantro | 16 shiitake mushrooms | ½ cup soy bean sprouts | 4 iceberg lettuce leaves | 4 sesame seed buns (page 18) |12 sliced pickled ginger from a jar | Salt and freshly ground black pepper*

④ 🍴 | M

③ Mix the mayonnaise with wasabi paste, sesame oil, sesame seeds, and coriander.

⑥ + ⑦ Wash the lettuce leaves and shake dry. | Cut the rolls in half, lightly toast the insides, and spread with the sesame mayonnaise.

BEAN SPROUTS

  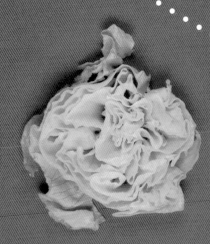

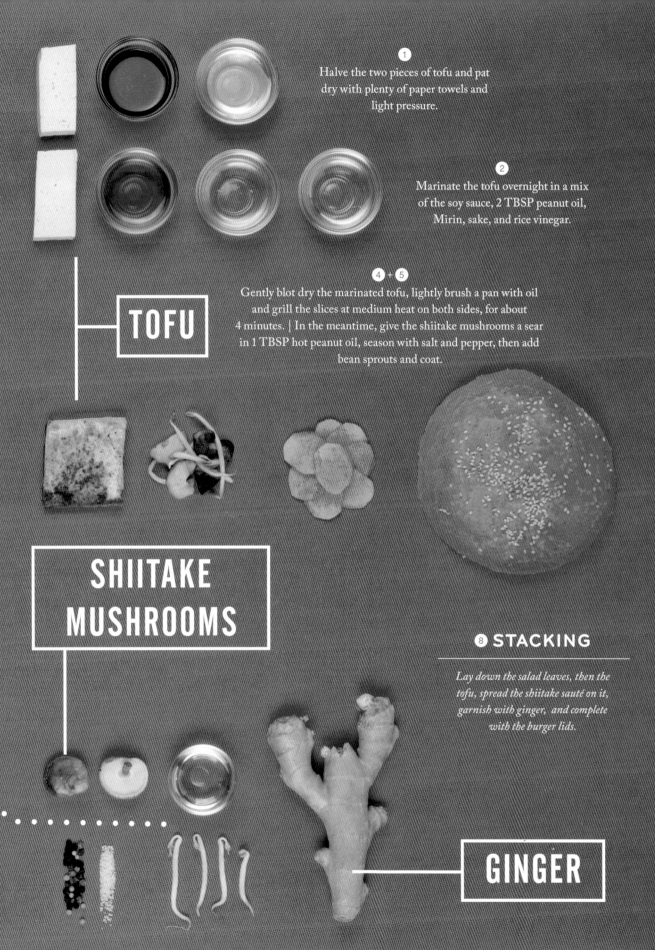

①

Halve the two pieces of tofu and pat dry with plenty of paper towels and light pressure.

②

Marinate the tofu overnight in a mix of the soy sauce, 2 TBSP peanut oil, Mirin, sake, and rice vinegar.

④ + ⑤

Gently blot dry the marinated tofu, lightly brush a pan with oil and grill the slices at medium heat on both sides, for about 4 minutes. | In the meantime, give the shiitake mushrooms a sear in 1 TBSP hot peanut oil, season with salt and pepper, then add bean sprouts and coat.

TOFU

SHIITAKE MUSHROOMS

❽ STACKING

Lay down the salad leaves, then the tofu, spread the shiitake sauté on it, garnish with ginger, and complete with the burger lids.

GINGER

BIG IN JAPAN

🐄 ④ 🍴 L

4 TSP GINGER
1 ½ LBS. GROUND BEEF
2 TBSP teriyaki sauce
1 TBSP ROASTED SESAME
1 PINCH OF SANSHO PEPPER (JAPANESE MOUNTAIN PEPPER)
½ CUP MAYONNAISE (PAGE 28)
4 TSP MISO PASTE (SOYBEAN PASTE)
1 TBSP YUZU JUICE (JAPANESE CITRUS JUICE)
1 BOK CHOY
1 TBSP SESAME OIL
1 TBSP SOY SAUCE
1 SMALL CARROT
¼ CUP WHITE RADISH
1 ⅓ CUPS OYSTER MUSHROOMS
2 TBSP PEANUT OIL
4 SESAME SEED BUNS (PAGE 18)
12 SLICES CUCUMBER
1 CUP SHISO LEAVES (JAPANESE HERB)
SALT AND FRESH GROUND
BLACK PEPPER

1 / Chop the ginger finely. 2 / Mix the ground meat with ½ TSP salt, teriyaki sauce, sesame seeds, sansho pepper and ginger mix, then form four equal patties, press a hole in the middles, and refrigerate for 1 hour. 3 / Mix the mayonnaise with the yuzu juice and miso paste. 4 / Preheat the oven to 350°F. 5 / Clean the bok choy and cut into rough strips. Sauté it in sesame oil, soy sauce, and white wine. 6 / Sear the patties on both sides in clarified butter and finish cooking in hot oven for about 10 minutes. 7 / In the meantime, clean the carrot and the radish and cut into fine strips. 8 / Sear the oyster mushrooms in peanut oil, add the carrot and radish strips, and season with salt and pepper to taste. 9 / Cut the buns in half, lightly toast the insides, and brush with the mayonnaise. 10 / Layer the bun bottoms with the bok choy, place the patties, spread the oyster mushroom sauté, lay the cucumber, garnish with cress, and top with the lids. ☛

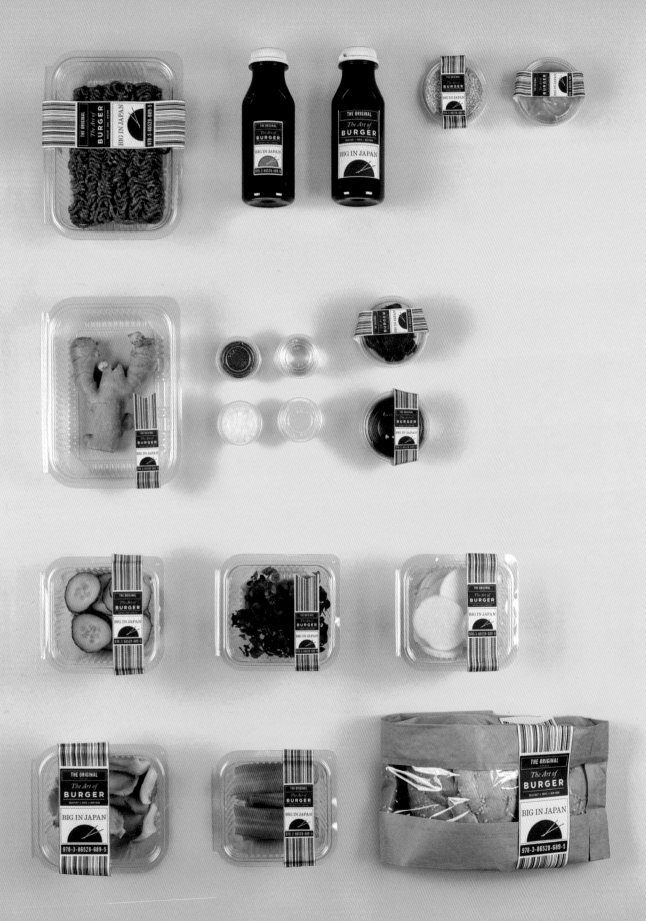

BOLLYWOOD

¾ cup plain yogurt (or sour cream)
2 TSP FRESH GINGER
½ CUP COCONUT FLAKES
1 ⅓ LBS. GROUND CHICKEN
I TSP GARAM MASALA (INDIAN SPICE BLEND)
1 TSP TANDOORI PASTE (INDIAN SPICE PASTE)
2 TBSP MANGO PUREE
1 PINCH CAYENNE PEPPER
4 POPPADUM (INDIAN LENTIL MEAL CRISPS)
4 LETTUCE LEAVES
4 CURRY-CHILI BUNS (PAGE 13)
12 SLICES CUCUMBER
SALT / OIL FOR DEEP FRYING
Clarified butter for frying

1 / Drain the yogurt overnight by hanging in cheese cloth. **2** / Dice the ginger finely. **3** / Roast the coconut flakes in a nonstick frying pan without any fat. **4** / Mix the ground meat with ½ TSP salt, garam masala, tandoori paste, ginger, and coconut. Shape into four equal-sized patties, press an indent into the middles, and refrigerate 1 hour. **5** / Mix the drained yogurt with mango puree and season to taste with salt and cayenne pepper. **6** / Preheat the oven to 350°F. **7** / Fry the poppadum in 350°C hot oil until golden and drain on paper towels. **8** / Sear the patties from both sides in hot clarified butter and let finish cooking in the hot oven for 10 minutes. **9** / Wash the salad leaves and shake dry. **10** / Cut the buns in half, lightly toast the insides, and coat with the mango yogurt. **11** / Put the lettuce leaves on the undersides, lay on the patties, spread the cucumber slices, garnish with the slightly broken poppadum, and finish with the lids. ☞

ORIENT EXPRESS

  4 ⑂ ⌐L⌐

CHICKPEAS →

CARROTS

YOGURT

❸ + ❹

Peel the carrots and grate finely. | Mix the olive oil and lime juice, season with salt and pepper to taste. Pour over the carrots.

❶ + ❷

Drain the yogurt overnight in a hanging cheese cloth. | Mix the drained yogurt with tahini and season to taste with salt.

5 — 9

Drain the chickpeas and blend in food processor. | Peel the onion and garlic and cut or chop into small cubes. | Chop up the cashew nuts. | Blend the chick peas with the onions, garlic, cashew nut, parsley, coriander, cumin, and harissa paste. Form four equally-sized patties. | Turn the patties in some bread crumbs and flour and fry on both sides in olive oil over medium-high heat for about 5 minutes.

ONION

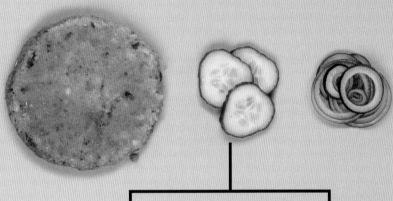

CUCUMBER

10 — 12

Wash the lettuce leaves and shake dry. | Peel the red onion and cut in rings. | Cut the buns in half, lightly toast the insides, and coat with yogurt.

12 STACKING

Place the lettuce leaves on the undersides and distribute 1 heaping TBSP carrot salad on top. Lay down the patties and garnish with cucumber and onion rings. Finish with the bread tops.

INGREDIENTS — ¾ cup natural yogurt | 2 TBSP tahini sauce | 2 carrots | 4 TSP olive oil | juice of 1 lime | 1 can chickpeas (about 1 lb.) | 1 small onion | 2 garlic cloves | 2 TBSP cashew | 2 TBSP chopped parsley | ¼ TSP cilantro powder | 1 pinch ground cumin | ½ TSP harissa paste | 3 TBSP bread crumbs and flour | 4 iceberg lettuce leaves | 1 red onion | 4 spiced buns (page 15) | 12 slices cucumber | Salt and freshly ground black pepper | Olive oil for frying

1001 NIGHTS

🐑 ④ 🍴 L

1 ½ LBS. GROUND LAMB
½ GARLIC CLOVE
1 CAN CHICKPEAS (1 LB.)
2 TBSP TAHINI (SESAME PASTE)
½ CUP OLIVE OIL
JUICE OF ½ LEMON
¼ TEASPOON CUMIN
1 PINCH CAYENNE PEPPER
1 AVOCADO
4 ICEBERG LETTUCE LEAVES
2 DATES
4 SPICED BUNS (PAGE 15)
½ CUP MAYONNAISE (PAGE 28)
2 TBSP HARISSA PASTE (SPICY CHILI-PASTE)
12 CUCUMBER SLICES
SALT AND FRESHLY GROUND BLACK PEPPER

1 / Mix the ground lamb meat with ½ TSP salt and ¼ TSP pepper, shape into four equal-sized patties, press an indent into the middles, and refrigerate for 1 hour. **2** / Peel the garlic clove and chop finely. **3** / Bring the chickpeas with their water to boil in a pot, then puree in a blender. Mix with tahini, 2 TBSP oil, garlic, lemon juice, cumin, and salt and cayenne pepper to taste. **4** / Preheat the oven to 350°F. **5** / Cut, core, and peel the avocado and cut into slices. Marinate with the remaining olive oil and salt. **6** / Sear the patties in a hot pan on both sides and finish cooking in the hot oven for about 8 minutes. **7** / Wash the lettuce leaves and shake dry. **8** / Cut the dates in half and remove the seeds. **9** / Halve the buns and lightly toast the insides. **10** / Mix the mayonnaise with the harissa paste and spread on the bottom halves of the buns. **11** / Place the lettuce leaves and 1 TBSP chickpea paste and cover with three slices of cucumber. **12** / Place the patties, cover with avocado, add another TBSP chickpea paste, half a date, and finish with the bun tops. 👉

5 Caramelize the remaining 2 ½ TBSP sugar in a saucepan, then deglaze with the remaining rum and pineapple juice.

6 Cut open the vanilla pod, scrape out the marrow, then add it into the saucepan and let it cook down into a thick mass. Marinate the pineapple cubes in it.

PINEAPPLE

1 – 3 Mix the flour with the baking powder. | Whisk the butter, ¼ cup sugar, and the eggs until foamy. | Bit by bit, alternately add flour and milk and add the 2 TSP rum. Let the dough rise for 2 hours.

4 Peel the pineapple and finely cube.

7 Preheat the oven to 325°F.

8 Mix the coconut milk, mascarpone, coconut liqueur, and vanilla-sugar, fill into a cream dispenser, add an appropriate gas cartridge, and refrigerate.

WAFFLE

INGREDIENTS — 2 ½ cups flour | ½ TSP baking powder | 5 ½ TBSP butter | ½ cup sugar | 3 eggs | 1 ½ cups milk | 4 TSP rum | 1 fresh pineapple | ¼ cup pineapple juice | 1 vanilla pod | 1/2 cup coconut milk | ¾ cup mascarpone | ¼ cup coconut liqueur | 1 packet vanilla sugar | ¼ coconut | 1 oz. dark chocolate | Grated peel of 1 lime | 8 mint tips

ARE YOU CRAZY?

COCONUT

9
Grate the coconut and roast in the hot oven for a few minutes.

10
Bake the dough in a waffle iron. Set aside 16 of the waffle hearts (waffle segments).

MINT

11 STACKING

Spread pineapples onto two separate waffle pieces, then add coconut cream, garnish with the roasted coconut and lime zest, grate some chocolate over the top, add some mint tips, and finish with the waffle tops.

RECIPE DIRECTORY

CAPITAL CITY *ground veal | veal liver | onion | apple* 50

SKYSCRAPER *boiled beef | potato | cream cheese | herbs | cucumber | egg* 54

CORDON BLEU BURGER *veal | asparagus | ham | Emmentaler or Jarlsberg cheese* 66

À LA NIÇOISE *ground veal | tuna | egg | onion | anchovies* 79

BENEDICT BURGER *ground veal | ham | egg | bacon | spinach* 108

PARIS PARIS *ground chicken | truffle | foie gras | plum* 71

THE BIG APPLE *duck breast | celery | walnut | apple | pineapple* 103

CLUB BURGER *chicken breast | bacon | tomato | cucumber* 104

CAESAR BURGER *turkey breast | Romaine lettuce | parmesan | anchovies* 106

GO YELLOW *ground chicken | orange | curry | lime* 118

BOLLYWOOD *ground chicken | yogurt | mango | ginger | coconut* 128

BROTHER JAKOB *scallops | spinach | peas | carrots* 69

BE HUNGRY—BE RICH *lobster | Serrano ham | seaweed | lime | avocado* 80

PRAWNY *shrimp | fennel | radicchio | olive* 93

CRAB ME GOOD *crab | bok choy | avocado | mango* 120

KÖNIGSBERGER *red beets | ground beef / veal | capers | anchovies* 48

BOY, COME HOME SOON *smoked pork | potato | pickled herring | red beet | onion | egg* 58

BISMARCK-BURGER *Bismarck (pickled) herring | egg | pickle | onion* 60

DANNEBROG *whole grain rye bread | kippers | onion | radish | egg* 63

À LA NIÇOISE *ground veal | tuna | egg | onion | anchovies* 79

TSAR NIKOLAJ *blintzes | salmon | smoked salmon | caviar* 96

CAESAR BURGER *turkey breast | Romaine lettuce | parmesan | anchovies* 106

AVOTUNA BURGER *tuna | wild herb salad | avocado* 123

BURGER WITH HANDKÄSE AND MUSIC *sour milk cheese | onion | apple | cumin* 41

HEALTH CITY *cottage cheese | cucumber | radish | sprouts | spelt* 56

CAMEMBURGER *camembert | cranberry | cress* 72

THE FAST (FOOD) SAMURAI *tofu | bean sprouts | shiitake mushroom | ginger* 124

ORIENT EXPRESS *chickpea | carrots | yogurt | onion | cucumber* 130

BERLIN AIR *doughnut | sparkling wine | raspberry | mint* 53

PEACH, WIND & CHOCOLATE *cream puffs | peach | chocolate | vanilla ice cream* 83

ARE YOU CRAZY? *waffle | pineapple | coconut | mint* 134

INDEX OF INGREDIENTS

HELEN HALL LIBRARY
City of League City
100 West Walker
League City, TX 77573-3899